Tell your sto

BRAD
COCHRANE

Story First Marketing

By Brad Cochrane

Story First Marketing

Author photo by Mike Nakamura

Dedication

For Bridget. At the end of the day, it's you.

Table of Contents

Telling Stories

Afterword

Appendix

Story First Marketing

Preface

Tell a fact to your customer and you trigger two areas of their brain. Tell them a story, and you trigger seven areas.

As a marketer, would you rather lead with a fact or a story?

Getting in front of your customer takes considerable investments of effort, time, and money. If your message fails to connect, what's the cost of that lost opportunity? How do you quantify the business that never was?

Story First Marketing engages your audience through an emotion-based story in which a brand, product, or point-of-view is integral to the story and its completion. It's a powerful approach to attract, engage, and move your customers to action through storytelling.

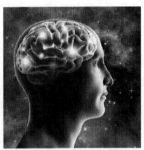

Romanova Natali –Shutterstock

I crafted this book so that you can acquire the knowledge, skills, and passion to use the power of Story First Marketing to transform how your customers think, feel, and act.

The Inside Story

The way you tell your story to yourself matters.

-Amy Cuddy

In the wind-swept plains of South Dakota, lies the humble community of Pine Ridge. On the Reservation, a young Oglala Sioux boy named Billy didn't have much of a future. But he could do one thing better than his friends. Billy could run. So he ran.

In the rarefied atmosphere of the 1964 Tokyo Olympics, nobody paid much attention to 26 year-old Billy. When the starting gun of the 10,000 meter race banged, Billy did what he always did, he ran. Before a stunned crowd, Billy Mills won his Gold Medal.
Hollywood even made a movie about him called *Running Brave*. Perhaps you've seen it. A young poor boy with determination gains glory, fame, and opportunity through relentless training.

U.S. Marine Corps

Years later on a sunny afternoon, I met Billy Mills at his tasteful elegant home. Well-respected, successful, and happy, he had come a long ways in life. Not every Olympic athlete is successful later in life and I was intrigued. What's the source of his prosperity? Certainly more than a single race? Billy chuckled; it all began with a story.

Before the explosion of the starting gun, before the relentless shock-shock-shock of the track beneath his feet, and before the splendid isolation of breaking the finish tape surrounded by thousands, Billy had run that race countless times before in his mind. He'd visualized himself crouching at the starting line, the feel of his soles hitting the track, the rhythm of his breath, the staccato of his heart, the slap of the finish tape on his chest, and the crowds cheering. Billy Mills created a story with texture and depth that he internalized for success. His story was so powerful, so familiar, that it simply couldn't be completed without him winning the race. Today this is a common technique for athletes but back in the 1960's, the idea was revolutionary.

That's the how, what of the why? Billy was a realist and knew that the world was bigger than Pine Ridge. He wanted more and if he couldn't change where he lived physically, he could change where he lived in his imagination. His desire for something different, whatever that might be, gave energy to his dream. He'd built within his mind a dream that was real and powerful enough to take Billy from the dead-end of his circumstance to the wide-open opportunities of the larger world.

Billy Mills had written a story for himself that overcame the relentless one-step-in-front-of-the-other training that he did every day through sun, wind, rain, and boredom. In that process, he'd learned to how write new stories for himself, stories that propelled him from the poverty of his birth to success, prosperity, and contentment.

He'd learned the secret of storytelling.

Why Storytelling?

In the marketing discipline, "storytelling" is a popular catchphrase that's overused, misused, and misunderstood. Stories themselves are frequently executed clumsily. Audiences are becoming wary because storytelling smacks of fiction, a well-constructed lie. Engineers in particular equate stories with fairytales. But great storytelling is honest, genuine, and true. And effective.

Stories are elemental to the human psyche. Stories are how people see the world, how they see themselves, and, most importantly, how people change themselves. Ideas are more powerful than things and storytelling is about ideas. Product features and data are really things, not ideas. So if we want our customers to embrace our product, then we need to use ideas communicated through storytelling.

My approach to storytelling is *Narrative Non-Fiction* in which facts are organized and presented in story form. It's similar to the television documentary that's so powerful for revealing truth and moving people to action.

SeaWorld is a popular amusement park famous for its performing orca killer whales. In 2013, the documentary *Blackfish* was released and focused on the tragic consequences of holding oracas in a captive environment. The public outcry led to decreased attendance, loss of sponsorships, and the eventual suspension of all orca shows. As narrative non-fiction, *Blackfish* revealed truth and moved people to action.

People often misunderstand storytelling. Some think that it's a lot of flowery words, some believe it's just entertainment, and some think it's a simple formula. But real storytelling ain't easy and takes knowledge, skill, and experience as well as a sense of balance. Story craft looks easy but is hard to master and demands work, practice, and a willingness for continuous learning. But the pay-off is worth every penny spent and every late night worked. By reading Story First Marketing, you're on the way to mastering storytelling to market your product, business, idea, or yourself and move your customer to action.

The truth is that we are all marketers and our products take many forms. If you're looking for a job, you're a marketer and the product is you. If you're a start-up entrepreneur, you'll need to raise money from skeptical investors and use the basics of marketing to do that. Perhaps you're a social activist out to change the world –ideas are the most potent marketing products of all –and sometimes just getting someone to feel differently is a powerful outcome.

What's my story?

I began my career in broadcast television. From soap operas to sports, from news to music videos, and everything in-between, I learned this lesson: television is telling stories.

Then I went into technology marketing. From demos to data sheets, from marketing pillars to product features, and everything in-between, I learned this lesson: customers weren't buying.

Why? Because we weren't connecting with our audience. We tried winning them over with data-filled over-rehearsed pitches but that's simply a one-way speech, a monologue, and not a conversation. We were talking *at* customers and not talking *with* customers. Our noise was drowning out our message. There was too much data and precious little listening. Customers weren't buying because they didn't trust how we were saying what we were saying.

Then it hit me. Rather than *story-yelling,* we should be *story-telling.*

From that day, I've committed myself to storytelling. From creative projects to public speaking to private consultations, I'm guided by these words:

My personal mission is to champion storytelling and its power to change how people think, feel, and act.

What is Story First Marketing?

I'm sure you've heard the advice to writers that a story has a beginning, middle, and end. Or a story involves a hero on a quest. Ask anyone and you'll get a different opinion. Here's my definition:

> *A story is a series of actions in which a sympathetic character confronts and solves a difficult problem while learning a greater lesson. The purpose of a story is to change the audience's internal state from non-interest to adoption of an idea; a story invites the audience to feel, be inspired, and act.*

Story First Marketing takes story a step further.

> *Story First Marketing engages the audience through an emotion-based story in which a brand, product, or point-of-view is integral to the story and its completion.*

The following tale is Story First Marketing at its best.

Derby's Story

Derby is a happy malamute with a quick smile and even quicker wag of the tail. He lives with his adopted family who loves him very much.

But Derby was born with deformed front legs which means that he'll never get to run and play like other dogs. Then one day, Tara Anderson met Derby and her heart opened up. She vowed to help Derby.

Derby already used a wheeled contraption for his front legs but it never worked very well.

3D Systems Press Kit

It just so happened that Tara worked for 3D Systems (which makes 3D Printers) and she brought Derby's story to the company. Everyone wanted to help and before long Derby had a new set of plastic composite legs made by the people at 3D Systems.

But unfortunately, the legs just weren't quite right. But that's the thing about 3D Printers, if the first prototype doesn't work, you can quickly redesign and make another set. Or another.

Well, it took three tries but today Derby has legs that let her run and play just like any other dog.

All thanks to a machine with skills and people with a heart at 3D Systems.

Derby's powerful story is told through an engaging online video. *(www.youtube.com/watch?v=uRmoowIN8aY)*. It's a powerful marketing message that's been seen nearly 9 ½ million times. You'll notice that the product isn't even mentioned until well into the story. I know that if I ever have a need for a 3D printer, I'm going to 3D Systems first. How about you?

As a viewer, our experience follows milestones along a path from start to finish:

1. **Engagement**. The story involves us through our curiosity and emotions. A dog without front legs is unusual so we're drawn in. Then, through the eyes of another, we imagine how awful that is and our hearts are touched.
2. **Problem**. With focused attention, we clearly see the problem and a need: Derby can't run and is incomplete as a dog.
3. **Solution**. Within this need gap, a solution is introduced by the 3D Systems product (which takes on the role of the hero to the rescue).
4. **Setback.** A struggle with creating the right prosthetics.
5. **Success.** With new legs that work, Derby runs free.
6. **Transformation.** As an audience, we identify with Derby, the people helping, and the product which are all inextricably entwined. Through our desire to help, to change the circumstances, we have changed inside.
7. **Lesson.** We've learned that to make Derby complete as well as ourselves, we need 3D Systems.

Of course, the market for helping dogs is limited but humans are flexible and can apply a lesson learned to new situations. Customers internalize the idea that when there's a problem that rapid prototyping solves, they want 3D Systems because that makes them a hero.

Storytelling is one of the best ways to teach positive lessons about how people successfully cope with the world, endure, and even sometimes win. The reader's satisfaction comes from learning with the character thus becoming a better wiser person.

The story of Derby is long and complex but Story First Marketing can be found in simple ads. Sometimes the stories are evocative, sometimes they're specific, and sometimes the story isn't linear. But the key here is that the completion of the story is dependent on the product; you can't have one without the other.

Public Domain

The Breakfast of Champions®. The iconic tagline for Wheaties breakfast cereal implies that to excel at sports, one must eat *Wheaties*.

With this phrase, a famous insurance company promises that after an accident, they'll make it right: *Allstate. You're in Good Hands*®.

The Hallmark greeting card company reassures customers that being a good person means buying cards from Hallmark: *When You Care Enough to Send the Very Best*®.

Nike's slogan *Just Do It*® encourages customers to be physically active by using their footwear products.

Public Domain

Salt soaks up humidity and tends to clump together in wet weather. The Morton Slat company solved this problem and celebrated their innovation with *When it Rains, it Pours*®.

A simple story can be expanded into multiple delivery systems. In a brilliant marketing campaign, the website purveyor Go Daddy takes their audience through a complex story journey across mediums that saves their pitch until the very end. Beginning with an ostensibly real TV ad for the *Cats with Hats* website, the viewer is left with the question "Is this for real?" Following up with a visit to the actual website, *Cats with Hats* seems to be a genuine business endeavor. However, scrolling to the bottom reveals the discovery of a clever put-on along with a powerful demonstration of how a business owner could be successful with Go Daddy. *(https://www.youtube.com/watch?v=q5pnIH9ZB2k)* *(https://www.godaddy.com/promos/campaigns/cats-with-hats)*

The purpose of Story First Marketing is to engage the audience around an idea, feeling or tangible product or service and stimulate awareness, positive perception, a trial, or a purchase. But more importantly, the desired outcome is that your customer advocates and evangelizes your product.

Marketing Today

Marketing today is a big mess. With more channels than ever before to deliver messages, the marketing environment is more efficient yet at the same time more chaotic. Information is becoming more and more de-bundled, that is, delivered in smaller chunks. Music that was once sold on record albums has de-bundled into individual songs and now parts of songs are sold as ringtones. The few print distribution channels such as newspapers and magazines have de-bundled into webpages, blogs, and tweets.

Marshall McLuhan famously said "the medium is the message" meaning that the delivery system influences and has a part in forming the message. In a digital world with on-demand just-in-time data, the medium conveys the message that information is to be consumed in the smallest slices possible and in any channel that is most convenient at the time. Instead of a knowledge construct that is built logically from beginning to end, knowledge aggregates itself as bits of data float by and stick. It's a difficult environment in which to organize a message, much less a campaign. Marketing can't keep up in this chaos and tends to take a scattergun approach. Success is measured through metrics with data that may be specious at best. As John Lennon once said, "How can I go forward when I don't know which way I'm facing?"

In this new audience environment, we're experiencing information overload. Messages stream into our senses in a constant cacophony of sight and sound from TV's, computers, phones, and devices. Take a walk down a city street and listen to the barrage. With all the noise, we struggle to make sense of it and practice defensive measures by limiting our attention. With every piece of new information, we need to make an instant determination if it's worth our time. And then decide how much time can we allow it. We work ourselves into an agitated sorting frenzy where our frustrated plea is to "just get to the point." As a survival tactic, we have trained ourselves to limit our time and limit our attention.

Marketers have responded in kind with shorter messages while shouting louder. There's a belief that communicators have only three seconds to get someone's attention. Some misconstrue this as needing to deliver their entire message in during that time. They talk fast becoming lost in the sea of noise. In actuality, marketers have three seconds before the decision has been made on *whether* to invest more time in the message.

Another strategy is to customize multiple messages with multiple strategies for multiple audiences. Just as one can't put out a fire with more fire, one can't calm chaos with more chaos. It's a game in which winning battles will not win the war.

Today's marketing environment has become a contest to see who can scream loudest in the shortest amount of time while rapidly cycling through features and benefits. While it's true that our audience is overwhelmed with data masquerading as information and they feel compelled to sort facts quickly, there is an opportunity to grab mindshare through stories that aren't constrained by the ticking of a timer.

In the business world, a company's decision to buy a product has evolved from a single person into a team. In an earlier time, software purchases were made by a computer engineer. In today's environment, a software purchase decision is shared by the CEO, CFO, and HR as well as the CTO each with their own opinion and need. Instead of marketing to the engineer with a single campaign, sales teams are targeting individual business interests using custom messages. The result is a flurry of proposals that aren't aligned in any meaningful way.

Storytelling is making a comeback because it has a competitive advantage over features-driven marketing; it conveys the big ideas that travel well across all mediums, channels, and audiences as well as communicating to all decision-makers equally. The responsibility of the storyteller is to get and keep attention so that the audience will turn the page. A good story has *legs* and can be told and retold in different forms. A *meta-story* has an overarching narrative that is told across mediums.

Big business is figuring this out. General Electric publishes the *GE Reports* online. With a relentless focus on storytelling, Editor Tomas Kellner has built a readership of 300,000.

At love's first blush, Mary and John spent every minute together. But alas, they parted, each to their home. So they did the next best thing to being in each other's company:

long phone calls talking until the talk runs out and the sound of the other's breath is simply enough. Yet it's not the same as being together because phone technology can't close the gap of human contact.

A face-to-face experience is High-Fidelity communication that engages listening, watching, and perhaps touching. Its action and reaction centered in sight, sound, and body language as well as sharing an environment of light, noise, smell, and temperature. High-Fidelity communication takes place in the realm of conscious stimulation as well as subconscious intuition. Whenever a technology is introduced into the communication path, some fidelity and clarity is lost. Although the telephone increases communication efficiency by aiding in talking across distances, it's not the same as being in the same room.

While every advancement in communication technology has enabled us to communicate in greater quantities, frequency, and immediacy, the quality of those individual communications has decreased. As communicators, we have drifted into a Low-Fidelity world in which we measure success by the number of actions rather than the quality of an individual interaction that is human and true.

The Low-Fidelity gap can be narrowed through High-Fidelity storytelling that stimulates senses, thought, and imagination. Although imperfect, qualitative storytelling is more effective than quantitative feature-listing because it's less affected as the technology degrades the message. As my printer friends point out, if one wants a better-quality copy, start with a better-quality original.

As mentioned before, instead of a purchase decision being made by a single individual, purchase decisions are now made by a committee consisting of stake-holders across a company. In the software market, technical experts have lost decision-making exclusivity. Business structures have evolved from a top-down hierarchy to flat organizations that seek consensus. So the target audience for any message is elusive and, in a sense, hiding in plain sight. A robust story speaks to everyone.

In the digital free-for-all with its spaghetti-like distribution paths, a great story engages your customer and keeps their attention on your product –a significant upside. We can make messages as short or as long as they need to be. Messages that used to be constrained to a 30 second commercial can now naturally expand into several minutes. In an environment of time-limited research, the customer is spending their scarce moments with your product rather than your competitor's. You've successfully staked out your claim in the audience's *mind-scape*.

According to the Harvard Business Review, statistics prove that companies that've embraced storytelling increase revenue and value by factors of four or more.

Another way of demonstrating Return on Investment (ROI) is an experiment that the Significant Objects group undertook which proves that storytelling adds real value. Using low cost items picked up at a garage sale, they offered an item for sale on the auction site eBay –something that people do every day. But the twist is that they created a story about the object to test if worth could be increased.

The *Kneeling Man Figurine* was purchased for $2.00 and Glen David Gold wrote a nifty little story about it. The result? The object sold on eBay for $56.50. That's a clear profit of $54.50. The story added perceived value as well as generating real cash.

Significant Objects

By the way, all profits were donated to charity.
(http://significantobjects.com/2009/08/04/kneeling-man-figurine/)

Once you recognize storytelling, you'll discover it whenever people get-together. Consider cosplay conventions in which enthusiasts dress as imaginary characters and bring to life magical heroes, evil wizards, or reanimated zombies.

Video storytelling is used to persuade others by revealing unknown facts and insights while modeling aspirational behavior. For instance, the personal diary video *Super-Size Me* follows the story of Morgan Spurlock who exclusively eats fast food for 30 days. The result on his body is disastrous. The film encourages others to make better food choices by demonstration.

In the world of commerce, businesses employ storytelling to create positive perception; an oil producer might portray themselves as good corporate neighbors. Smart entrepreneurs develop a narrative that keeps them on track while a job seeker leverages storytelling to connect to hiring officers. A salesperson will use a powerful story to lead a customer through an objection and to a sale.

A great story is like touching sticky fly paper. The audience is immediately involved, engaged, and paying attention. The experience, as well as a gluey finger, lingers on into the future. Anyone else who touches fly paper has a similar experience and so everyone's thinking is aligned around a shared story. A story in which a character is made personal to the audience teaches and models behavior, leads to an internal state of change, and stimulates action.

In all the shouts and noises of modern marketing, we've lost storytelling and with it a loss of meaning. People are hungry for stories. Storytelling builds customer relationships which leads to trust –the ultimate coin of the realm in business.

What is Data First Marketing?

The year was 1998 and the future looked bright. By all accounts, the Rio 300 internet music player was a technological breakthrough and a sure-fire bestseller. The Diamond Company staked their future on miniaturizing a portable music player that exploited the developing digital technology and the internet. The early adopters were enthusiastic.

Where is the Rio 300 today? Relegated as a historical side note. Although the reasons for its ultimate failure are complex, it's worth taking a look at the marketing approach. This magazine advertisement is a feature-filled data sheet which appeals to the analytic side of many early adopters but  doesn't mean that much to a general consumer market. Diamond, an engineering company, marketed to themselves. This is Data First Marketing in which the product leads, features follow, more data is added, and there is no real call-to-action. It's an unmemorable message that the average person tunes out.

Three years later, Steve Jobs walked on to the stage to introduce an exciting new breakthrough in music: the Apple iPod. A small portable internet music player exploded onto the scene and heralded a seismic culture shift in how we listen to music as well as the music industry itself. Why did the iPod succeed while the Rio 300 failed? The reasons are complex but the story first approach to product development and marketing lies at the core. *(www .youtube.com/watch?v=kN0SVBCJqLs)*

In Steve Jobs' presentation, he takes the audience on a journey that is both personal and universal, aspirational yet grounded in facts. He opens with the statement "Music is universal" appealing to the creativity in us all. Having set the stage, he delves into the market, product, and features while interweaving personal stories throughout. In every example, he leads with a story and then follows with features. With the phrase, "All your music fits in your pocket," he then proves it with facts. The messaging approach is Story First Marketing in which a story of a personal experience is backed up by the product features. With an appeal to imagination, an effective story results in an internal change of state and stimulates a call-to-action that can only be completed with the product.

More than just a marketing phrase, the storyline drives the product development itself. The Apple team aligned themselves around "fits in your pocket." From an engineering perspective, this meant 5GB of flash memory to store 1000 songs. The device had to be small enough to fit inside a pocket and, in fact, Steve Jobs pocket; he slipped a wood prototype into his jeans every morning and rendered a verdict at the end of the day.

Apple understands that a wearable device is a fashion accessory –people are very particular about their wardrobe. Headphones at that time were plain, large, and clunky making them unattractive to the fashionista so inconspicuous earbuds became a must. Finally, the device has to be simple to use because nothing should get in the way of the music experience so an innovative interface emerged. Story first, features follow.

Before purchasing the product, the customer first adopts the internal belief: *To be cool, I need the Apple iPod.*

mylerdude (Flickr)   Aaron Logan   Pixabay.com

Data First Marketing is ubiquitous because a product maker's natural inclination is to sell to themselves; it's who they understand. In this case, the marketing message becomes disconnected to the customer. A marketer who can bridge the gap creates value for both the product and the customer.

The Human Story

Humans are wired for story.

–Garr Reynolds, Presentation Zen

The human experience is story. It's how we learn about life, the world, and ourselves. Stories entertain while teaching us positive lessons about how to successfully cope with the world, endure, and win. We gain personal satisfaction by identifying with characters as we learn with them to become better, wiser people.

Stories are how we share a common culture that brings us together and aligns a greater purpose. Stories have been told since the dawn of mankind and are everywhere, in everything and in everyone. In the Bible, Moses goes to the mountaintop, meets a burning bush, and returns with the Ten Commandments. The story bonded an ancient nomadic people together into a religious cultural tradition that has lasted many thousands of years. In ancient China, a politician philosopher brought together a divided people into a common cultural identity through the power of moral stories. Today, we know Confucius through his sayings that extoll the virtue of doing the right thing at the proper time. Those that know the Golden Rule, *What you do not wish for yourself, do not wish unto* others, know Confucius. Stories can be regarded as the original technical manuals that teach people how to live and thrive.

At the other end of history, modern Americans watch the Super Bowl on television. Ostensibly a sports contest between the two best teams in the National Football League, a fair number of TV viewers watch it for the commercials. Some are clever, some are not, but they're all entertaining. Talking about Super Bowl commercials is a cultural event in which we gather our new common stories. (In fact, people will take a bathroom break during the actual game so they don't miss the commercials). Although sitting around a campfire has evolved into posting on Facebook, the desire to share stories is still strong, a part of who we are.

As a toddler, my son often asked "How did you and Mommy meet?" He wanted to know where he came from, why he was here. It's a story he wanted to hear over and over as he sought to make sense of the world. Children need lessons on how to behave so we teach them through stories: *Actions have consequences: sometimes desires and sometimes undesired.* Isn't that the essence of any story?

Plato's Cave, as recorded by Socrates, is explained as a conversation between Plato and one of his students. Plato relates the experience of prisoners chained inside a cave that can only see shadows cast by their guards; this is their world and their only understanding. One day, one of the prisoners is released and brought outside into the world of light, color, and movement for the first time. The philosophical question proposed is this: how does the released prisoner go back and explain the real world to his former fellows? Does he use rational facts and data that they have no context for? Or a story employing symbolism that explains the unfamiliar in familiar terms? *Plato's Cave* is an allegory about how stories can be employed to lead others from the darkness of ignorance into the light of greater understanding.

The Human Brain

The intuitive mind is a sacred gift and the rational mind a faithful servant. We have created a society that honors the servant and has forgotten the gift.

—*Albert Einstein*

The human brain is the apex of evolutionary progress, the creator of art, philosophy, and technology. No other animal brain is smarter. It's also really, really dumb.

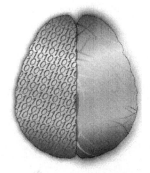

Sam Cochrane

Why? The human brain can't see, it can't hear. It can't taste, smell, or touch. It only knows what it knows through neural impulses sent by the sensory organs of the eyes, ears, and nose. Depending on the signal received, different areas of the brain are activated. The thinking process evaluates, categorizes, and aggregates incoming information to create knowledge, experience, and memory. In the Left Brain – Right Brain Theory, logic is processed within the left side of the brain while emotion is processed within the right. The Human Brain integrates logic and emotion; it seeks balance and completeness.

In traditional education, students are drilled on facts through rote memorization techniques. The idea is to repeat numbers, dates, formulas, and facts enough times so that they "stick" in memory. For the non-data minded, it's a painful process of hammering one part of the brain over and over. Numbers, facts, and data have little meaning by themselves; 88 has no significance other than it's one more than 87. It's a teaching approach that appeals to logic.

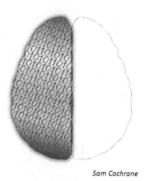

The Left Brain (or Logical Brain) is a check-list maker that's good at organizing numbers, facts, and data. According to brain expert Scott Schwertly, facts and statistics trigger just the two areas of the brain that process language comprehension.

Sam Cochrane

With any incoming messages or sensory input, these parts of the brain are asked to make a judgement, to agree or disagree. As a defensive strategy against the daily barrage of information, the brain seeks yes or *no* answers; it's focused on *no's* more than *yes's* as a way to keep the list clean.

For the Left Brain, proof wins arguments. In the context of marketing, product features have to check every single box on the checklist; a brimful of facts is not enough.

If a marketer leads with data, the Logical Left Brain is triggered and the message is more likely to be sorted into the wastebasket of the mind. Likewise, a litany of data points depresses overall brain activity as only two areas of the brain are triggered. Is it any wonder that the most common folk remedy for sleeplessness is to count sheep?

The Right Brain (or Aspirational Brain) is an adventurer that seeks new experiences and embraces possibilities. Again, according to Schwertly, a story triggers seven areas of the brain including those that process language comprehension, colors and shapes, scents, sounds and movement. With any incoming message or sensory input, the brain is asked to participate. The Aspirational Right Brain is more likely to say *yes* because it sees the possibility of the product

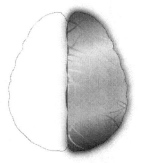

Sam Cochrane

By leading with story, the Aspirational Brain is triggered and, this is key, the product experience becomes real, the customer can imagine themselves using it –thus leading to desire and eventual purchase. Stories win decisions.

Add context to numbers, facts, and data to make them meaningful. The number 88 becomes significant when paired with the revelation that a modern piano has 88 keys and the first rock and roll song was named *Rocket 88*. More areas of the brain are activated and that number becomes memorable.

The Pavlov's Dog Experiment is a famous inquiry into behavioral conditioning. It begins with the observation that a dog naturally salivates when offered food. If a bell is rung at the same moment every time, the dog begins to associate the sound with the food. Eventually, the ringing of the bell alone is enough to trigger the salivating response. This experiment had great implications in the field of behavioral science but it's also relevant to why stories are effective. Remember that the brain only knows what comes in through its neural pathways so even a description of a sensory experience such as a smell or sound will to some degree seem real to the brain and can stimulate in almost the same degree as the real thing. Cheeseburger anyone? Stories wake up the brain.

Specificity leads to memorability. That's why writers are encouraged to use detailed sensory descriptions becuase it triggers as many parts of the brain as possible thus making the story seem more real.

For instance, compare the power of "the air smelled bad" to "the acrid air bit his nostrils." Did your nose just crinkle? Mine did. *Embedded Simulation* refers to the idea that imagining an action stimulates the same part of the brain that actually carries out that action. The mental imagery that Billy Mills and athletes use has been shown to stimulate specific muscle groups. The goal visualization used for self-improvement and personal empowerment as shown in the movie *The Secret* has proven itself successful. The famous acting coach Lee Strasberg developed an acting technique in which an actor fully creates and develops a character by tapping emotional memories inside themselves. The *Strasberg Method* has given us some of our greatest actors including James Dean, Dustin Hoffman, and Scarlett Johansson. A powerful Embedded Simulation can pass the threshold from imagination to memory, that is, an event being remembered as real whether it actually occurred or not. The good news is that you don't have to train like an athlete, guru, or actor; words also stimulate the same part of the brain.

Stories are both ephemeral and tangible, emotional truth and hard facts. Sight, sound, smell, taste, and touch are sensory inputs that travel as electrical impulses between nerve cells to the brain where a pattern is stored. The pattern then triggers any number of responses such as no action, immediate action, or referred action and the details go into short term memory or long term memory. As more sensory inputs arrive, they're added to the existing memory patterns. By evaluating patterns, insight and learning takes place in the brain's natural quest for meaning. Meaning attracts meaning and the resultant pattern is stronger and more prominent because of the additional connections to other patterns. So if we can attach meaning to a product through storytelling (which stimulates multiple parts of the brain), then the overall pattern becomes stronger and more prominent. If that pattern includes an action dependent upon our product, then the brain will attempt to complete that action.

One could argue that the easier path for the brain is to *buy* or complete the product action as it matches a pre-existing thought pattern. If another action (or inaction) occurs, than the brain has to reconcile the two thought patterns. Perhaps this is why that a mind once made up is hard to change. If a decision is made and imprints a pattern (and I argue that the decision is made on the aspirational level), then new incoming data is sorted to match the existing pattern. The goal of a marketer is to make that thought pattern as robust and deep-set so that thoughts and actions conform rather than destroy the pattern.

In a sense, an embodied simulation is like a movie in the brain, an imagined experience that exists only within. It's a very powerful construct in that an embodied simulation will stimulate the same parts of the brain as if the experience were real. For instance, visualizing a delicious dinner can make mouths water and induce hunger. By turning the product into an embodied simulation, the brain will attempt to replicate that simulation at a later date through a purchase.

Vivid stories with powerful language can trigger the senses to create a full-bodied experience that seems real to the brain. Relevant descriptions engage the listener. For a sports enthusiast, stories that include the home team are more interesting.

A message with just words, such as a blog, isn't nearly as effective as adding a picture because the message is now engaging two different encoding processes in the brain. Adding sound and movement engages the brain exponentially. Video storytelling is more effective than other mediums because moving imagery imprints directly into memory as an embodied simulation. It's almost like being there in the story.

Recording a video is simple while video storytelling is an art and craft unto itself. Quick cuts, splashy effects, and hard-driving music doesn't replace storytelling. Viewers can be attracted with shiny visuals but there must be a purpose.

The most effective way to create an embodied simulation is to have the customer try out the product. A real experience naturally becomes a memory and motivational driver. That's why auto dealers encourage test drives. And a good salesperson will hand a soft sweater to a customer to feel. (Once the sweater is in their hands, it usually ends up as a purchase). Real estate agents light cinnamon-scented candles to make an open house feel more like home. Stimulated senses create more robust embodied simulations.

An embodied simulation plays a functional role in understanding. People often replay an argument with a spouse or partner over and over in their mind as they try to understand what happened. Or perhaps remembering vivid dreams as details take on greater meaning in the morning light with a realization that the images represent something more. (Chasing a giant rabbit symbolizes a striving for success).

The Metaphorical Simulation or the *This is like that* idea helps us to use a lesson, or emotional insight, as a cautionary tale that can be applied to another situation for understanding. We can choose to embrace a new thing or avoid it depending what we have learned elsewhere. For example, the phrase *free like a puppy* reminds us that we need to aware of the overall cost of a purchase rather than its original price. A boat's monthly docking fees, fuel, repair, and insurance eventually costs more than the original purchase price. The phrase *devil in a blue dress* reminds us to look past the surface beauty and beware of underlying character. On the other side, there are metaphors that lead us to good things. *Stop and smell the roses* reminds us to enjoy life for life's sake. A fable, or story with a moral, can teach us life lessons that can be applied to new situations. The

Tortoise and the Hare with the moral *slow and steady wins the race* reminds us to keep at the task.

A memory is an embedded simulation that can trigger feelings that are good or bad. (Although we'd rather forget the boss chewing us out). Pleasant embedded simulations can stimulate us to future actions as we try to recreate that feeling associated with it.

On a personal note, I'm a snow skier who loves schussing through fresh untracked snow –a powder hound. One particular morning, I looked from the top of the Heavenly Valley ski area to Lake Tahoe below. It had snowed 14

Connor Wallberg via Flickr

inches the night before but now the sky was clear and the sun shone through a thin forest of pine. The flakes were light, the air crisp, and the angle of the slope just right. I pushed off into the untracked powder in long graceful arcs that went from left to right and back again. But the most vivid memory is floating upwards in the apex of the turns and drifting down at the end experiencing a weightless rhythm where I was one with the snow, myself, and the universe. Rarely does one have such peace. Ever since, my skiing career is devoted to recreating that moment, that memory, that embedded simulation and although I've had wonderful runs that stand on their own, I can still feel the windburn on my cheeks, the cool taste of dancing snowflakes, and see the dappled light on smooth crystal-white snow as if it were right now.

On the dark side of the street, recovering addicts will frequently describe their downward journey as they chased the memory of their *first high*: the original moment of drug-induced perfection. Subsequent drug use fails to reach anything like the first high but that didn't stop them from trying. Or perhaps someone in an abusive relationship clings to the memory of how wonderful it all was in the beginning. Memories are powerful and can be more real than reality.

The goal of a great story is to create an embodied simulation so that the listener will think, feel, and act. The writer doesn't have to get it completely "right" but just have to be close enough as the mind will fold in the facts. In fact, it may be the brain's ability to understand without complete information that drives curiosity and desire to complete a story.

Storytelling is much more powerful than data but there is a place for proof. Facts and data are essential reassurance that adopting an idea or product or point-of-view is the correct decision logically. The logical brain is compelled to double-check, compare, contrast, and test. Facts impart credibility as well as proving the decision to others such as your boss or spouse.

The Martian by Andy Weir tells the story of an astronaut's survival on the planet Mars. The overriding story rule is that every scientific principle and technology the castaway uses to stay alive must actually exist today (or in the proposal stage). There're no magic genies that blink their eyes to save him. It's hard science fiction in the best sense taking the reader on a journey from the Logical Left Brain

rain to the Aspirational Right Brain and back again. Story and facts.

Confirmation bias is an assumption, viewpoint, or belief that is deemed to be true and, because of this mindset, subsequent facts are rearranged to align with the original belief. If your customer has come to a conclusion based on their immersion in your story and supporting facts, they will defend their decision to the end. The Logical Brain rationalizes emotional decisions. A person rarely disagrees with their own opinion.

Let me give you a personal example from when I bought a new car. After numerous visits to different showrooms, I sat inside in a blue Jeep Cherokee and knew that this was the one. I can't describe how I knew other than I felt "cool." So I bought it. As I parked my new ride in the driveway, a neighbor wandered over. "New car, huh? Why'd ja' buy it?" I couldn't articulate my subconscious desire or justify a gut feeling so I recited facts and figures about gas mileage, towing capability, and resale value. But deep down I knew I had made an emotional decision which conflicted with the rational part of my mind. Buyer's Remorse creeped in until I was able to reconcile the two halves of my brain and honor the emotional as well as the rational.

Story First Marketing creates an equilibrium by using story to trigger and engage multiple parts of the aspirational brain while still feeding facts and data to the logical brain, The Left Brain focuses on what *is* while the Right Brain focuses on what *could* be. Because the brain seeks

Sam Cochrane

completeness, a story balanced with facts can sell across the human spectrum.

The brain is inspired by aspirational visualization so inspire your audience. Lead with story and the facts will follow.

Have you ever tried giving a cat a bath? I have and wear the scars to prove it. As a child, we lived in the country and every summer the county would spray down the gravel roads with tar. One hot humid morning, Mom yelled at us kids to stop tracking tar onto her freshly-waxed linoleum floor. Looking closely at the offending marks, I saw the pattern of tiny tar footprints that led directly to our newly acquired black cat –eating contentedly at his bowl. Tarball! The moment I dangled the oily-scented cat out over the washtub, Tarball's legs splayed out with extended claws and his yowls pierced the country stillness. My friendly little kitten exploded into a scrabbling, scratching, hissing, black ball of fury doing everything he could to avoid the water below.

Pixabay.com

Make your story Tarball, sticky, scrabbling, and digging in with everything you've got to avoid being dipped into the brain's washtub and rinsed into oblivion. Fight with skill, talent, and passion and be *remembered.*

Ethics in Storytelling

Authenticity reinforces trust in what is real in an
increasingly staged, contrived, and mediated world.
-James H. Gilmore, New York Times interview

Truthfulness isn't the absence of lies; it's being true to underlying character, personality, or spirit. Authenticity is actuality, realness, and trustworthiness. Storytelling isn't an opportunity to lie.

The truth of the matter is that lying doesn't work. The brain is a highly evolved organ that excels at spotting lies and recognizing fabrications. It uses both a rational process to verify facts as well as an intuitive process in which something presented doesn't "smell right." People will see right through a falsehood damaging your brand, your product sales, and possibly your career. According to the New York Times, 63% of customers buy brands that are seen as more authentic than its competitors and 60% recommend organizations they see as authentic.

Humans are complex organisms and a multitude of emotions lie within the psyche: fear, love, delight, hope, and more. Marketers easily fall to the temptation of playing on emotions but not every marketing story should be a sad tear-jerker. There's an elemental difference between using crass sex or appealing to a higher ideal: get the beautiful girl or save the planet. As The Comedy Coach® Neil Liebermann advises, "A stand-up comedian can get an easy laugh with a dirty joke but is it the *right* laugh?"

Honest marketing is more effective and viable than dishonest marketing which, although garnering immediate sales, is unsustainable over the long run. Predictably, false notes manifest themselves in dissatisfied customers, word gets around, and profits fall more than was originally gained. More to the point, the entire brand and product can be irretrievably damaged.

The advertising company McCann-Erickson's slogan *Truth Well Told* has been in use for over a hundred years. To quote from their home page:

> *We believe Truth is a catalyst for authentic ideas, powerful ideas that will be believed, embraced and advocated by people in their everyday lives.*

Lofty sentiments indeed but underneath lies a practical guideline for ensuring that your marketing messages are authentic and effective.

Examples of inauthentic marketing abound. It usually happens when someone decides to imitate a successful campaign without understanding the underlying truth that makes that campaign genuine.

The underlying mission of the Starbucks coffee company is to provide what they call the *Third Place*, a space where the community comes together to share. Their stores are one part coffee shop, one part workplace, and one part home. In 2014, a massive landslide destroyed the village of Oso in Washington State. As news came into the surrounding communities, first responders sprang into action. Not far behind, the manager of a nearby Starbucks, on his own initiative, brewed coffee and personally delivered it to rescue personnel *because that's what a community does*. That's a powerful authentic story.

Every now and then, you'll find a company that promotes a virtuous value but its actions fall short. It may be a charitable organization that uses most of the donated funds to pay for fancy offices and high salaries. Or an airline that fudges with arrival times to increase their official on-time ranking. Or a company that advertises great customer service but condemns customer calls to helpline hell.

Why do we believe one organization's claims and not another's? Actions that are in alignment with a company's core values tend to be perceived as authentic.

Political propagandists use psychology and an understanding of the group mind to tap into hidden motivations and exploit those for their own purposes. These techniques are not far removed from modern advertising so it becomes a personal choice on how marketers participate. Is the motivation to provoke reactions in people for the sake of the reaction or is it to provoke a reaction to stimulate greater understanding and positive action? Is the point to stimulate negative feelings such as hate, anger, and fear? Or positive feelings such as love, kindness, and confidence?

In the end, you must have personal conviction in your story. When your message and your internal belief system are aligned, your audience can sense authenticity even if they can't define it consciously. If you are lying to yourself, you are lying to everyone.

About Stories

Story Basics

An object at rest stays at rest unless acted upon by an unbalanced force.

-Newton's First Law of Motion

At its very essence, a story can be described as *physics in action*. A character resting in a stable state is transformed by an outside force and learns an important moral. See what happens to the hero of *Egged On*...

There once was a happy little egg. But one day, the evil Hand snatched Egg from his comfortable carton and cracked him open over a hot frying pan. As he hit the hot greasy surface, he curdled in sizzling agony but the happy little egg remained optimistic. He firmly believed that in adversity, a good egg always keep his sunny side up!

Pixabay.com

Although a silly story, there's a serious lesson as the character goes through four stages. First, the egg is in a stable state, whole and unbroken. Second, the hand, acting as an outside force, cracks the egg over the hot pan. Third, the egg is transformed by heat into a delicious breakfast. Fourth, a moral about optimism is revealed.

For purposes of storytelling, the stable state can be thought of as **Context**, the outside force as the **Complication**, the transformation as the **Result**, and the moral as the **Lesson.** So, our story breaks down as follows:

1. **Context**: Egg is whole and happy
2. **Complication**: Hand cracks Egg into hot frying pan
3. **Result**: Delicious egg breakfast
4. **Lesson**: Stay optimistic in adversity

The *What happens next?* question is the *Curiosity Gap* that keeps an audience interested. Remember, that as humans, we seek completion. A slot machine challenges our curiosity with a spin of the wheels and rewards us if we've guessed the right result –a jackpot. Video games are a never ending expression of Context, Complication, and Result.

Here's an example of a simple story that takes place in prehistoric times.

Meet Grok. Grok has a rock. Meet Crick. Crick has a stick. Grok throws the rock at Crick. What happens next? Perhaps the rock hits Crick. Or the rock misses Crick. Maybe Crick swings the stick... and misses the rock... or hits the rock to send it flying.

Shutterstock

What really happens in this story? The game of baseball is born. The action on the field and the progression of the game to the final score is an expansion of the basic story of a ball and a bat and what happens next. The uniforms, stadiums, 7th Inning stretches, rivalries, and contract demands are merely embellishments all based on the Rock & Stick Game.

With added complexity and details, a simple basic story can evolve. In fact, a test of robustness is that the story can be told in new ways and styles. For example…

Showdown on Flatfield
By Brad Cochrane

Beware the smile of a beautiful woman; it can change everything.

After many cold suns, our tribe had arrived at Flatfield for the long days of summer. I picked up rocks from underfoot while the others cleared brush. I looked over to Crick, who already had claimed the best cave for himself, and his mate Reeka. She smelled of rotted deer and dirt, a fragrance no man could resist.

She walked with purpose, tough and beautiful, leaving me roiling in her wake. Reeka smiled in a way that communicated more than the grunts and clicks that passed for our language. In that moment, we both knew what had to be done. I would kill Crick and claim his woman and cave for my own.

Crick must have sensed my desire for Reeka. With a growl, he turned and waved a freshly broken branch at me.

My hand clenched tighter around the rock in my hand. With a screech, I threw the rock straight at Crick. He waved his stick again and the rock hit it bouncing through the air like a bird and directly back at me. My eyes are good and I ducked as the rock flew by me. Fluttering on, it hit Reeka in the head killing her.

My sorrow for my poor dead Reeka was great. I let no one move her so the tribe covered her where she lay with dirt and stones. She lies under a fine mound and I stand atop it guarding her day after day. Whenever Crick comes close, I throw stones at him which he hits with his ever present club. Knowing that I'll never leave my Reeka, he taunts me and runs round my mound and back to his cave, back home.

The tribe watches us with great enjoyment, encouraging one or the other of us with yells and cheers. The young ones imitate us and have begun to throw rocks and swing sticks at each other. To keep them safe from hurt, the elders have begun to put rules on their play.

In my dreams, I see the children of the tribe playing the rock and stick game long after I am gone. They wear strange furs made from the same animal and swing cleverly fashioned sticks at rounded white rocks. The watching tribes are many, beyond the counting of my hands, and sing a song of happiness as one.

All summer long, we've been at it and with the turning of the leaves, it's time for the tribe to leave this place. A truce between us has been declared by the elders until we return to Flatfield next spring. But I will kill Crick.

There's always next year.

Stories are **consequence** –from the Latin *with, to follow*.

Stories are action, something has to happen. A chase, a journey, or an escape are common action plots. Although great stories have been told from the perspective of a person trapped in a prison cell, bed, or under a rock, action takes place no matter how small. In the movie *127 Hours* James Franco's character, pinned by a boulder, relives his past adventures in flashbacks, ponders his relationships in memory, and hallucinates a future – the trapped person escapes his confinement if only in imagination. For a story to have sufficient action to hold interest, there has to be a significant investment in physical or psychological effort.

In this same way, a story has to have action that is clear, that makes us work a little (or at least go along for the ride) and leads us into the satisfying task of completion. There is a sense of accomplishment in having been integral to the action that solved the problem.

Stories are **emotion** –from the French *move the feelings*.

Someone has to feel something and be changed because of that feeling. Curiosity draws the audience in and empathy keeps them watching. The approach is to engage interest, increase involvement, encourage identification with the character or situation, evolve as a person, and experience an internal change of our point-of-view.

As favorite Mad Man Don Draper says, "You are the product. You… feeling something. That's what sells."

AMC.com Press Kit

Stories are action and emotion. Action movies can leave us empty inside while sentimental movies can feel pointless. *Transformer* movies explode off the screen but lack emotional calories. *Downton Abby* drenches historical atmosphere but aside from a missing silver spoon now and then, not much really happens.

Stories take the audience on a journey through time and space as well as a journey of personal enlightenment. A powerful story changes us inside in profound ways. Although it has the familiar Beginning, Middle, and End, at its heart a story is Context, Complication, and Result.

Story Structure

A song starts in a place, tells a story, and ends with a feeling.

–Kenny Rogers

Hyacinth –Wikipedia Creative Commons

Like a musical score with beats, notes, movements, and rhythm, a story has a structure that guides action, direction, and momentum to a desired conclusion.

There's no single all-encompassing story structure but rather variations that take differing paths. Each writer has their favorite approach.

A story structure has turning points, places in which the story takes a new direction. For instance, screenwriters swear by just two turning points: the first is a complication of the main character's life and the second when that character gains understanding and the tools to solve the original complication (although not necessarily a return to the original life they had). It's the simple story of Context, Complication, and Result.

Choose from the following Story Structures for the one that works best for your story.

Did you know that writing a good Hook increases reader interest by 85%?

Now that I have your attention… A **Hook** is that first bit of communication that engages the reader and makes them want to read more. It's advertising for the rest of the message. There's no one way to write a Hook –some suggest a question, startling fact, or mystery. A great Hook is part magic, part science, and part luck but it always leads the reader from their own world into another. For a newspaper headline, it might be "Baby Missing," for a Dickens novel it might be "It was the best of times, it was the worst of times," and for a web page look no further than "The 12 best celebrity bodies; you won't believe number 7!"

Journalists structure their reports using the **Inverted Pyramid** in which the most newsworthy information is listed at the top followed below by details in descending order of importance or immediacy. It's a convention suited to newspaper reporting with the assumption that the reader will not necessarily read the entire account. Its focus is the classic *Who*, *What*, *Where*, *Why*, and *How* order of information.

AFDPO

However, it's not storytelling in the sense I use but rather reporting –an important distinction.

The **Generalized Story Structure** has 7 turning points:

Generalized Story Structure	
1	Hook
2	Familiar
3	Surprise
4	Set-Back
5	Struggle
6	Success
7	Lesson Learned

The late Joseph Campbell taught **The Hero's Journey**. It's most famous adherent is George Lucas who used it as a model for the original *Star Wars* movie. At its most basic, The Hero's Journey is a circular story in which the main character leaves home on a search, encounters allies, achieves success, attains a reward, and returns home. Of course there are set-backs, struggles, and lessons to be learned along the way.

The **Story Mountain** is a journey of increasing difficulty until success is attained and the reward is won. It's common in action films in which car chases, fights, and explosions repeat getting bigger and bigger until the hero vanquishes the villain or the filmmaker runs out of budget.

1. Struggle
2. Success
3. Setback
4. (Repeat)
5. Reward

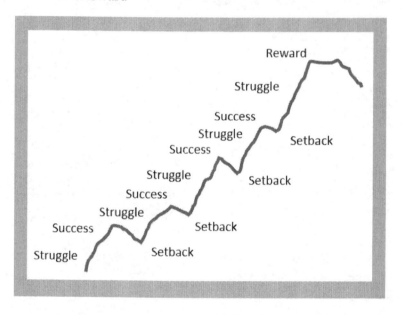

A great example of the Story Mountain is a TV commercial for the Chevrolet Silverado pick-up truck. *(https://www.youtube.com/watch?v=eZUNEhE- Xw)* The story borrows from the TV show Lassie in which a smart courageous dog saves his family. The Silverado plays the role of Lassie and humorously overcomes ever increasing odds by saving the family from a water well, runaway hot air balloon, shark attack, and volcano. Just when the story couldn't get any more outrageous, it does. The lesson: *if you need a truck, you need the Silverado.*

Another way to look at story structure is the **Turning Point Diagram** which shares similarities with the Story Mountain.

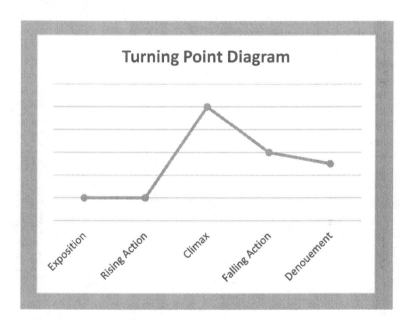

Turning Point Diagram

Exposition Rising Action Climax Falling Action Denouement

We all love a good puzzle and the **Mystery Story** satisfies that part of the human brain that enjoys teasing apart clues to discover a solution. It's why crossword puzzles, Sudoku, and the latest episode of CSI are so popular. In the classic mystery, the crime happens first. Then the investigation unravels the threads of the crime with the help of clues. It's a parallel story in which the story of the crime is paired with the story of solving the crime; a race between the readers and writer; the reader to figure out the solution while the writer delays the *revelation* as much as possible. There's an element of the unexpected and then fun in seeing how it all fits together.

The Mystery Story graph below charts the involvement level of the Criminal and Detective as the intertwined stories move left to right from crime to solution. The Criminal and Detective cross paths as one pursues the other and eventually come together in a final confrontation.

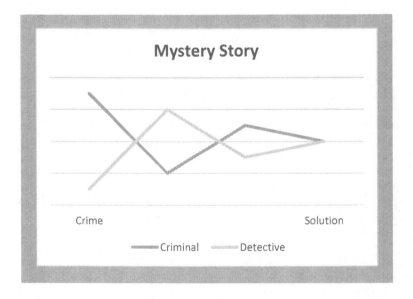

Stage 1. The crime takes place. The Criminal is most involved. The Detective, unaware, is least involved.

Stage 2. The Detective, aware of the crime, begins investigating while the Criminal hides. It's not unusual for them to cross paths.

Stage 3. The Detective enters a period of introspection while the Criminal, believing he is safe, emerges and may even take further action.

Stage 4. The Detective and Criminal meet in a final confrontation where all is revealed.

Jokes are a type of mystery story. In the comedy profession, much of the humor comes from surprise and then the joy of figuring out why something is funny. In practice a good comedian doesn't telegraph the *punchline,* that is, tell the end of the joke before the beginning as it spoils the experience for the audience.

Although we generally use words, pictures are also a great way to tell stories. However, the photo you use shouldn't be too obvious. With some subtlety, we can engage our audience as they try to puzzle out the mystery.

In this photograph of business executive Dale King, photographer Rick Dahms was asked to include the logo of the business; not an unusual request. Depending on the shape, logos are easy to fit in and sometimes not. Rick cleverly used only parts of the logo in multiple places within the photograph as well elements that only suggest.

Rick Dahms

The audience has to tease out the logo. Instead of a standard business photograph, we have a picture that engages the brain with a mystery, a solution and a memorable name: Tacoma Rail.

I've developed **Cochrane's Story Table** to design my stories. The story moves through multiple states of being, actions, and changes underpinned by setbacks, successes, and twists.

Cochrane's Story Table

Hook	*Lorem ipsum dolor sit amet, consectetuer adipiscing elit.*
Context	*Lorem ipsum dolor sit amet, consectetuer adipiscing elit.*
Characters and Setting	*Lorem ipsum dolor sit amet, consectetuer adipiscing elit*
Complication	*Lorem ipsum dolor sit amet, consectetuer adipiscing elit*
Motivating Incident	*Lorem ipsum dolor sit amet, consectetuer adipiscing elit*
Set Back	*Lorem ipsum dolor sit amet, consectetuer adipiscing elit*
False Success	*Lorem ipsum dolor sit amet, consectetuer adipiscing elit*
Twist	*Lorem ipsum dolor sit amet, consectetuer adipiscing elit*
Result	*Lorem ipsum dolor sit amet, consectetuer adipiscing elit*
Final Twist	*Lorem ipsum dolor sit amet, consectetuer adipiscing elit*
Lesson	*Lorem ipsum dolor sit amet, consectetuer adipiscing elit*

These are just a few of the story structures available. Use the one or ones that feel most comfortable and appropriate.

The **Story Plot** is different than a Story Structure. Plots have specificity within the variations of story structure, that is, descriptions applied to story structures. It's similar to saying that a house has a structure of a floor, wall, door, and roof but that the plot determines if it's a castle, split-level ranch, cabin, or tent. For instance, the story structure could be laid out as struggle and success but the plot could be a rags to riches story, slaying a monster, or even a farcical comedy. The story itself furnishes dramatic details.

Throughout history, writers have attempted with limited success to quantify the number of available plots. The number ranges from one to thirty-six depending on how a plot is defined as well as personal preferences. For example, Christopher Booker investigated the literature from a Jungian psychological perspective and declared Seven Plots.

1. Overcoming the Monster
2. Rags to Riches
3. The Quest
4. Voyage and Return
5. Comedy
6. Tragedy
7. Rebirth

I'll leave it up to you to make your own analysis.

Story Dynamics

In a conventional sense, a character is the person who's affected by a complication, acts, and resolves problems to reach a state of equilibrium. But a character can certainly be a place or thing; it sets rules for what the story will or won't do. In the *Star Trek* universe, the heroes are Captains Kirk and Picard but the *Starship Enterprise* is itself a strong character that represents adventure, curiosity, fair-play, and resilience within the larger character of the Federation. Character is important because it sets a consistent tone that the audience comes to trust.

Within the story structure are story dynamics that tug and pull at character creating internal conflict and motivation. To use the analogy of a wooden sailing ship, the sails pull against the mast which is held back

Pixabay.com

by rigging ropes that strain the hull which creaks and cracks as it fights the waves. If character is the ship in dry-dock, then the story dynamics are the struggle of the ship at sea as it journeys to its destination. The ship must do so within the constraints of the rules of its world, that is, it can't ignore the wind, the waves, the physical limitations of its wooden construction, or the organization of the crew. The essential conflict is that between the stability of character and the forces intent on destroying stability. The character has to be at risk or the tension isn't compelling enough to be worth caring about.

The Story Dynamics are…
- ➢ Connection
- ➢ Tension
- ➢ Rhythm

Within the created story world, connections between persons, things, the situation, and action are ever changing as each one reacts to the other. The audience's interest in the state of the relationships and the tension as they push and pull is what brings a tale to life. Throughout the story, new connections can be revealed and seemingly important ones fall by the wayside. A character should always be connected to the situation and action as well as physical objects. There's a truism among playwrights that a gun introduced in Act 1 must be fired by Act 3.

Tension is the anticipation that hovers between a complication and result. I mentioned the Curiosity Gap earlier and the audience's need to know "What happens next?" is powerful. In a well-crafted story, the audience becomes the story and is engaged by internalizing the tension and behaving as the character would –or should. They scream when the zombie's hand breaks through the door, smile when the girl finally gets the guy, and cry quietly when the underdog wins the singing contest. They're relieved when the tension finally breaks as the result destroys tension. Adept writers are very careful to create the next tension quickly to drive the story along.

Tension, which is physical or emotional and sometimes both, keeps us interested but must ultimately resolve the complication. What is the real result? Is it attaining a reward or the moral learned along the way? In some way, the result must complete an important action or lesson.

In 1914, Sir Earnest Shackleton prepared an Antarctic expedition that would cross the South Pole. He had a plan, a ship, and supplies. Legend has it that this advertisement appeared in a London Newspaper.

Pixabay.com

This appeal is powerful because it stimulates anticipation in the readers. Imagining themselves as an intrepid explorer, the ad inspires customers to engage in an upcoming activity especially if it takes commitment and effort on their part. Wondering what comes next, they are held in a state of tension until the story is completed.

I call this technique *Once upon a time in the future…* with an implied call-to-action to participate in a story yet to be written. It can be as straightforward as *Baseball Game Tonight!* with the implied call to come and see your team win (or lose). Or as consequential as Shackleton's ill-fated expedition in which his team became trapped on the ice for nearly two years. But at the time that this ad appeared, the story was simply *Once upon a time in the future…*

A great example is the TV game show *Wheel of Fortune* which uses two levels of tension. In the first level, the giant prize wheel is spun and the audience waits in anticipation to see if the pointer lands on cash, prizes, or a bust. In the second level, the player has a chance to solve the puzzle by guessing the secret phrase. So great is the human need to resolve tension that the audience competes to solve the puzzle before the player.

If a story is like a song with beats, notes, and movement, then rhythm is its pace and velocity. It can move with relentless energy or linger over each note. Rhythm regulates the speed of the journey and models the internal behavioral state that audiences experience whether it's fast or slow, anxious or calm, or something in between.

Rhythm responds to connections and tensions making the overall story stronger or weaker. A boy and a girl that fall in love too quickly aren't believable just as a love story that takes too long. Rhythm chooses the right moment.

A story is word choices. It might be selecting a delivery style that enunciates in precise clipped tones or alternatively a style that rolls along in studied laziness. A story is what's said explicitly as well as the gaps left to the imagination. A story is sound and silence, a choice between a loud shout and a quiet whisper. A story is a living dynamo breathing energy that waxes and wanes within the story structure to give it direction and purpose.

The Marketing Story

If you would persuade, you must appeal to interest rather than intellect.

-Benjamin Franklin

The ultimate objective for a Marketing Story is to create one or more of the following states in the customer:

1. Awareness
2. Belief
3. Adoption
4. Confidence
5. Advocacy

Before a customer can buy a product, they have to be aware of it. In the Derby the Dog story, the first state is *awareness* of 3D printing and the 3D Systems Company. The second state is *belief* that the product is credible, that it can do the job. Introducing a case study is very effective as it models the product in action and endorsement by another customer. But that doesn't necessarily mean that the customer will enter into the third state of *adoption* of an idea or product. This is where the power of storytelling and the aspirational brain can move the audience as they imagine themselves in the story. Almost by the necessity to complete the story, they adopt the product through a purchase. Although money may change hands at this point, the sale isn't really completed until the customer reaches the fourth state of *confidence* in the decision they've made. This is where data, facts, and features reassure the logical brain. The fifth and final state is *advocacy* for your product, that is, encouraging others to buy. Advocacy is the best proof that you've successfully led the customer through the previous states (with the added bonus of increasing future sales).

Some marketers get caught up in their own cleverness and tell stories that are very witty but have little to do with the product or customer. On need look no further TV commercials that leave viewers amused but wondering exactly what product is being advertised.

Remember…

The audience experiences an internal change.

The product is integral to completion of the story.

Understanding the larger audiences' background, culture, and values is key to any marketing message. Yet, the audience is complex and made up of individuals. More important than gender, occupation, and income are their emotional aspirations or desires. And just as important is understanding where a specific audience member is within the sales cycle. The end goal may be the purchase of a product but the immediate need can be a quite different but necessary step in the process. Satisfying a current need clears the way for forward progress.

Consider the real service you're providing to your customer and how they see you. Your role in their lives is more than selling them a product and moving on. My accountant Charlene Fleming understands that her role isn't only filing taxes (easily done with software) but is really about keeping her clients calm throughout the process.

Companies frequently invest in great products that no one actually wants or needs. Sometimes it seems that no one's asked the customer their opinion. For instance, Gerber, the baby food company, wanted to expand into a new market segment: single adults. So they relabeled their iconic glass jars of baby food with the new name *Gerber Singles*. To say that sales were disappointing would be an understatement.

And sometimes a flawed study will give erroneous results. In 1985, the Coca-Cola Company was fighting for market share against the sweeter tasting Pepsi. They ran a series of taste tests comparing a new sweeter formulation against their traditional formula and the results were overwhelming; people preferred the sweeter taste. New Coke was introduced to the world –and flopped. What Coca-Cola had neglected to consider was how the new formula tasted after the second, third, and forth sip; New Coke was too sweet. Coca-Cola returned to the original formula soon after. Remember, the only customer survey that counts is the sales tally.

The bottom line is to make sure that what you're offering is what the customer needs –not what you think they need.

A marketing message needs to address the immediate needs of a customer to open the way for the eventual purchase. Recognizing audience context is key. Is the customer an investigator, decision-maker, or lookee-loo? Do they want information, a solution, or entertainment? Is their current state skeptical, open, or disinterested? What are their needs, stated and unstated? What do they think they need? Is there an opportunity to shift their perception to what they really need? A better understanding of the audience leads to better targeted stories that are more appropriate for the customer and situation.

How does the audience interpret the world? It's essential to recognize the cognitive style of your audience. For instance, engineers tend to like receiving information in chart form because they are visualizers. Others prefer text because they are verbalizers.

In any case, get to the point quickly. Conciseness, which elevates salient points, is different than summarization, which conveys all top-level points. Beware of compression which squeezes everything into a short amount of time.

Consider the generational style of your audience. Baby Boomers, Generation X, and Millennials all have preferred styles of communication. My son, who's a Millennial, and myself, who's a Boomer, present a humorous talk on communicating across generations. It grew out of an exchange we had via texting that went something like this:

Son: Hi Dad! It's been awhile since we've talked. Want to catch up on a phone call?

Dad: Fine.

Son: The new apartment is pretty good but I have a question about the crock pot you bought me.

Dad: When?

Son: Are you free at 6:30? Or any time after that...

Dad: 6:30.

Son: Why are you so angry with me?

Of course I wasn't angry but in my worldview texts are useful for communicating essential information in as few words as possible. For my son, texts are part of an ongoing larger conversation with friends and family. A short answer to him is abrupt, rude, and angry.

We use emails differently too. I send long detailed messages and engage in conversations. For my son, his email service is where he stores reference information such as class schedules, agreements, and instructions. With this insight, I now know why he never responds to my emails but will converse with me via text messaging.

Although the Marketing Story stays the same, the delivery methods have to adapt to your audience. Matching the style of communication leads to better understanding and retention of the message.

Post-War America experienced unbridled optimism and prosperity. Automobiles became a popular *must have* for every family. In response, roads were built at a breakneck pace in response; paved US Highways crisscrossed the country. However, cars were mainly used for errands around town. The dilemma for automobile manufacturers was how to speed up the purchase cycle, that is, how to make the product wear out faster so they could sell their customers a replacement. The answer? Encourage more driving the way Chevrolet did in this perfect example of Story First Marketing.

Public Domain

The story, *See the U.S.A.* arrives first. It's an aspirational story in which the audience sees themselves participating. Who wouldn't want to visit exotic places, leaving cares behind, in the safety of one's own back yard? The product, *your Chevrolet* follows second and visually details the features of make and model. The preposition *in* is the aspirational activator that puts the customer into the scenario and makes the product essential to the completion of the story. A customer internalizes the belief "I want to see America so I need this reliable car."

The story informs and aligns the additional visual elements such as the binoculars, highway sign, historical marker, and the panorama of the open country, and mountains. There's also a secondary story, *See your local Chevrolet dealer*, which inextricably pairs the adventure story with the outfitter who makes it possible. As a final touch, the advertisement is in the shape of a license plate further reinforcing the story with a tangible automobile feature.

To review, stories are an external journey with structure, action, and completion as well as an internal journey of emotional completion in which the audience feels, learns, is inspired, and changes while learning an important moral lesson. The odyssey from complication to resolution changes the character profoundly and also changes the audience through their identification with the character. The resolution comes not from the closing action but rather from the enlightenment or lesson that solves the real problem.

Fables

One approach to create strong marketing stories is to use a fable as a template. By reverse engineering a fable into its component moral, that moral becomes the basis of a new marketing story.

Fables teach a moral lesson or illustrate a point. By observing the result of an action, an insight is gained into that action or an innovative solution is revealed through a universal lesson: the moral. (A good fable teaches multiple lessons).

The following tales demonstrate how an ancient fable can be translated into modern marketing by use of the connecting morals of *everyone matters*, *treat others how you want to be treated*, and *be prepared*.

Fable

The Bundle of Sticks

The old King lay near death and gathered together his many children. "Who shall have the kingdom after I'm gone?" he asked. "I'm the oldest!" said one and another said "I'm the cleverest!" So it went as each child made their case. Then the King held up a bundle of sticks and asked each to break it in two. None could. Then he separated the sticks and broke each one in turn. "You must all work together to keep the kingdom safe" said the King and closed his eyes for the last time.

Moral

Everyone matters

...because they bring their own strengths.

Marketing

United Negro College Fund

A mind is a terrible thing to waste.

The UNSF provides scholarships for African-American students as well as those in need. Promotes itself and services though media advertising. The tag line's moral lesson is that everyone matters and can contribute to society.

Fable

The Lion & the Mouse
One day, Lion caught Mouse in his big paw. Mouse
pleaded with Lion to release him and promised that he
would help Lion someday. Amused, Lion released Mouse.
The next day, a net fell onto Lion trapping him. Lion
moaned in despair. "Don't worry" said the small high
voice of Mouse, "I'm here." Mouse then chewed through
the net freeing Lion. Ever after, Lion and Mouse were fast
friends.

Moral

The Golden Rule
...treat others the way you want to be treated.

Marketing

Les Schwab Tires
My Les Schwab Story
A chain of neighborhood tire stores in the U.S. Northwest,
Les Schwab is well known for friendly service that goes
the extra mile. In this campaign, customers relate their
own positive experiences.

The Ant & the Grasshopper
"Come out and play," said Grasshopper to which Ant replied, "Not today, I'm gathering food for the winter." Grasshopper skipped away and played.
Sometime later, the weather turned cold. As Grasshopper shivered towards death, he said "I should've gathered food when I could."

Be prepared
...for the future.

Allstate Insurance
Mayhem
The character Mayhem takes delight in damaging automobiles, homes, and lives. Accidents can't always be avoided but Mayhem's destruction can be repaired by purchasing Allstate Insurance beforehand.

Using fables as a template for marketing stories works because they both appeal to our universal humanity. In these examples the fables aren't literally replicated, an ant doesn't drive a car, but the moral lessons emerge loud and clear. Fables cross cultures and time.

For instance, say that management believes that productivity could be improved if all employees felt empowered to make decisions. A marketer is asked to find stories within the company that support this idea. Asking employees outright if they have power to act will garner a variety of responses –not all of them good. However, if the fable *The Bundle of Sticks* becomes the centerpiece story, then the moral "Everybody matters" drives the research, interviews, and narratives.

Here's a real world example for a marketing video that I wrote and produced: Windows Intune is a Microsoft product that enables IT Administrators to manage computers remotely in such a way that bypasses the need to physically take possession of the hardware. I profiled the charitable organization *Save The Children*. Their IT Administrator was frustrated that he's always behind in managing his network; Windows Intune solved his problem. Yet instead of creating a straightforward case study of facts and features, I began by telling my client, crew, and interviewees the following fable by an unknown author.

The Sleeping Farmhand

There once was a farmer who needed a farmhand. One day, a young man came to the door and the farmer hired him on the spot. As an afterthought, he asked the farmhand what he did best and was perplexed when the young man answered "I sleep when it rains." The days passed and the farmer was well pleased with the farmhand's work as the fences were straightened, the livestock well-cared for, and the old barn roof patched. One night, a terrible storm descended on the farm. Jolted awake, the panicked farmer ran out to the barn and slipped inside. The animals were quiet, the wind muffled, and the barn dry. He then heard snoring coming from the farmhand's bunkroom and understood that because of the diligent foresighted work, the farmhand sleeps when it rains.

The video itself began with the **Context** that *Save The Children* has a mission is to provide health services, housing, and education to the planet's neediest citizens: children. To do this well takes the help of worldwide staff whose computers are supported by the IT department. The **Complication** is that the laptops are difficult to manage and can only be updated when they are physically at headquarters –an infrequent occurrence. It's a haphazard affair and the IT Administrator is frustrated because the process gets in the way of providing quality service. Enter Windows Intune which solves the problem by enabling the IT Administrator to update computers whenever connected to the internet. The **Result** is that *Save The Children* is back to its mission of saving children.

Before a single frame of video was recorded, *The Sleeping Farmhand* explained the video's purpose and aligned everyone's efforts on what, how, and why. By internalizing this story, everyone involved understood that the real story was about the IT Administrator who through careful preparation became the hero. Although not a single word of the fable was used in the final video, interviewees articulated their understanding with phrases like "eye in the calm of the storm" and "When people need help, they're going to get it from us."

Where do we find the stories that inspire and teach us to be better marketers? The gems are in plain site to be picked up. Classic stories are a treasure trove of moral lessons that can be translated into effective marketing stories. Every marketer should read Rudyard Kipling, Aesop, Mark Twain, and James Thurber as well as Sherwood Anderson, Jean Shepard, and O. Henry. Read more to write more.

More riches are buried in a quieter past when marketers could concentrate on stories that were as long as they needed to be. My personal inspiration comes from a discarded book picked up in a garage sale for fifty cents. In *The 100 Greatest Advertisements* written by Julian Lewis Watkins, I found the stories that moved customers to action and the stories of how the stories came to be. If you're looking for inspiration, seek out this book and others sources like this. Learn from the masters and master your craft.

The Five Storylines

Whether you are a marketer promoting a product, an entrepreneur pitching to investors, a job seeker meeting with a hiring officer, or a social activist trying to change the world, there are Five Storylines that need to be developed. In any interaction, all five may be told, sometimes just one, but it's usually a mixture depending on the circumstances. Think of your marketing effort as a tapestry and the Five Storylines as threads woven within that give it design, color, and substance. Sometimes you'll use one thread, other times two or three, and sometimes all five. It depends on the tapestry you want to weave and the story you need to tell. Fully develop all five and use them when needed.

Remember, whether selling a product, yourself, an idea, or a point-of-view, it's all about marketing. But to be clear, a storyline isn't a fictional lie but rather a vehicle for delivering a truthful message that is authentic and honest.

Five Storylines for Marketers	
1	Core Storyline
2	Credibility Storyline
3	Experiential Storyline
4	Journey Storyline
5	Data Storyline

Communicate to others the way in which they want to be communicated.

The Core Storyline

Connect with what gets you excited and great things happen.

-Matthew Bennett

On July 20th, 1969 Neil Armstrong stepped onto the lunar surface and uttered "That's one small step for man, one giant leap for mankind." Humanity's dream of going to the moon had at long last come true. Important words indeed but

NASA- Neil Armstrong

not as momentous as those of President Kennedy nine years earlier, "We choose to go to the moon. Not because it is easy but because it is difficult." Without those first words, we'd never have heard the second. Kennedy's speech is the Core Storyline that guided actions, resources, and subsequent storylines. His clear directive drove the design of rocket ships, science education, NASA, national pride, and human achievement (as well as the citrus drink Tang). All the budget battles, project management techniques, training, and personal sacrifices are just details to the Core Storyline, "We choose to go to the Moon."

A few years after Kennedy's speech, President Johnson visited the Kennedy Space Center and happened upon on janitor with a mop. When asked his job, the janitor replied, "I'm putting a man on the moon, sir." Although most likely apocryphal, there is real truth in that the hundreds of thousands of the Apollo Program workers felt the same way.

The Core Storyline is usually short, to-the-point, aspirational, and powerful. It's a meta-story guides all efforts and informs all marketing. It's the zeal and purpose that drives actions; the *why* behind the *what* as Simon Simek might say. The Core Storyline is an aspirational quest, a Hero's Journey that is yet to be completed. A Core Storyline is spare, repeatable, and robust so that it can easily be passed to others with understanding.

Marketers caught up in product development, research, financial estimates, advice free-for-alls, and metrics will frequently lose sight of what they are doing and why. When asked about their product, they'll data-dive into features and price-points. A strong Core Storyline at the beginning will keep marketing on track through the ups and downs of a campaign while reminding the business of their underlying passion when they need it most.

For job seekers, an authentic Core Storyline kick-starts the search, drives forward momentum, and props up sagging confidence. It sets a direction to navigate within an overwhelming maelstrom of unknowns.

A Core Storyline is developed by digging down to the basic ideals and then articulating specific goals using an active, aspirational, and clear voice. The Core Storyline is *doing* and not a statement of fact –a verb and not a noun. It's "We choose to go to the Moon" rather than "We are the recognized leader in space travel." It avoids the passive description and embraces the active Core Storyline that has an ending yet to be completed. The Core Storyline itself is fixed but execution allows missteps and course corrections that lead to eventual success. The Core Storyline illuminates the path forward; it's a proactive declaration and not a reactive statement.

A slogan isn't a Core Storyline. Sometimes they can use the same words but a slogan is specifically a short salient memorable phrase that advertises a product. A slogan is about catching attention and not necessarily about a guiding a product or company towards a goal. For instance, the Nike shoe company's Core Storyline can be paraphrased as "We inspire and support athletes to do their best" while their slogan is *Just Do It!* –certainly related but not the same.

A strong Core Storyline can be a slogan as well as the name of a business. For instance, *Food 4 Less* is the name of a grocery chain, slogan, and Core Storyline all wrapped up into a memorable phrase. My book *Story First Marketing* and associated talks, workshops, consulting, and content creation falls under a single moniker.

A few short years after Neil Armstrong's historic walk on the lunar surface, the United States abandoned the moon. The public, politicians, and media had lost interest. Kennedy's story had resolved itself, the driving tension between his aspirational words and the fulfillment of our collective dream dissipated in the swirls of the astronauts' ticker-tape parade. The Core Storyline had been lost and a new one had not yet been found.

Compare "NASA: We're going to the Moon!" to "NASA: We're developing deep space exploration technology and through a series of carefully planned missions performed on a vague timeline, we will eventually land a person on Mars!" Which narrative is more powerful as an organizing principle for rocket ships, budgets, and people?

Pay Pal and Tesla entrepreneur Elon Musk has a personal vision of humans colonizing the planet Mars. To that end, he's started his own space venture Space X. So far, Space X has developed rocket technology that has successfully resupplied the International Space Station, landed the 1st stage of a rocket after launch, and, as of this writing, is on track to launch astronauts into space. As anyone in Space X will tell you, every celebrated victory is just another stepping stone to Mars. The Core Storyline is "We're going to Mars!"

The Core Storyline shouldn't be confused with a Mission Statement although they're very similar and nearly identical. A Mission Statement details what the company is and not necessarily where it's going. Mission Statements tend to be wordy and written in a passive voice that sounds like a legal document. They're good for large multi-faceted companies where the goal is to communicate unity to a large number of customers, shareholders, and employees.

This is my Mission Statement from an earlier time:

Brad Cochrane is a professional communicator who consistently delivers compelling narratives for marketing and business. In a world of competing messages and information overload, Brad puts order to chaos and specializes in helping people, products, and businesses find and tell their unique and authentic stories.

The typical Elevator Speech usually crams facts into a thirty second spiel, again, what has been. Unfortunately, more isn't better. My earlier Elevator Speech:

> *I'm a professional communicator delivering compelling narratives for marketing and business. I put order to chaos. I specialize in helping people, products, and businesses find and tell their unique and authentic stories.*

And my new Core Storyline:

> *I champion storytelling because I believe in its power to change how people think, feel, and act.*

Compare these examples. Notice that my original Mission Statement is passive, wordy, and unfocused; it tries to do too much and comes to a hard stop. At social events, when asked to introduce myself, I recited my Elevator Speech, a shortened version of my Mission Statement, as fast as I could. No wonder I inspired glazed eyes and a desire to escape to the appetizer table. On the other hand, my Core Storyline is active, succinct, and focused. It encourages more conversation as I'm asked about storytelling –which then leads into Story First Marketing. Personally, I believe that Mission Statements and Elevator Speeches should really be a Core Storylines that're written in an active voice to stimulate further conversation.

A strong Core Storyline that's authentic and specific keeps everyone focused; vague words equals vague results. If the product description reads like a laundry list of features, then any change in those features nudges the message off track. A strong Core Storyline leaves room for the business to adapt and not be tied to a specific technology.

A Core Storyline is a great way to motivate a large organization towards a specific goal. As a bonus, the skills learned from executing one Core Storyline can have beneficial results in other aspects of a business.

I once interviewed Secretary of the US Treasury Paul H. O'Neill who recalled his time as CEO of Alcoa Aluminum. Back then, Paul had a problem. The company was a mess and losing ground. People lived in fear, didn't trust each other, kept to themselves, and avoided collaboration. Paul recognized that unless he got everyone working together, the business was doomed. The usual appeal to increase profits wasn't a motivator for the staff to change behavior. Besides, that'd been tried before and no one believed that working harder would benefit them in a personal concrete way. But Paul was a smart fella and realized that even if people wanted to work together, they no longer knew how.

Paul created a new Core Storyline of *Zero Injuries*. By placing workplace safety as the first priority of the company, Alcoa communicated that as a group, "We care about each other, we are in this together, and we will put aside our differences to work for a greater good." The results? Predictably, safety-related injuries dropped dramatically. More importantly, as employees worked across business units and hierarchical roles on newly formed safety teams, people learned how to work together in an environment of openness and trust. The organization as a whole became more efficient as new ideas flowed freely and everyone felt that they were respected. Unpredictably, except to Paul, profits, market share, and stock value soared. By the time Paul left 14 years later, Alcoa's market value increased by a factor of 9 and annual net income increased by a factor of over 7. Not bad for a Core Storyline that's not about profits.

From Silicon Valley to Seattle to *Shark Tank*, entrepreneurs are pitching their ideas to investors. Despite conventional wisdom, the way to an investor's wallet is not through facts but through storylines well-told. In my work with entrepreneurs, I've recognized a familiar pattern: an entrepreneur has a flash of insight and births an idea that can change the world. Excited and with a clear goal in mind, they start the journey of developing their product. Then the helpers get involved with well-meaning advice. Financial wants to know the ROI, Legal wants to create contracts, and everyone else has an opinion. By the time the entrepreneur gets a meeting with an angel investor, the original insight has been turned on its head. The entrepreneur pitches numbers, data points, features, and any and all sorts of logical arguments but can't understand why the money guys aren't interested. The real reason? It's because angel investors aren't in it just for the money. I'll say that again: angel investors aren't in it *just* for the money. To be clear, they'll diligently investigate the financial viability of any proposal. But they want to change the world and are looking for others who want to do the same. They know that the secret to success is to partner with entrepreneurs that have a clear idea of why they are doing what they are doing. An entrepreneur should tell a strong truthful story to illuminate the answers that investors want. As time is limited, it has to be to the point. Investors respond to a clear Core Storyline.

Entrepreneurs tend to invent a product first and then try to tack on a story on later; marketing is seen as a final step in the process rather than the first step. I recently advised an entrepreneur who was developing an app that helps drivers in the event of car trouble. His product description detailed the user interface, connectivity, and software features. I challenged him to dig deeper and after numerous iterations we worked our way to a Core Storyline of "When your car engine bursts into flames, we keep you from freaking out!" Instead of focusing on the technical details, the new Core Storyline keeps his business focused on how to best serve his customer regardless of what may come in the way of technological hurdles, market changes, or even legal limitations. It opens up possibilities rather than closes them off.

Products should be built around a solid narrative. A strong Core Storyline at the very beginning focuses the design approach, business organization, and product execution into a successful endeavor. A great Core Storyline resists drift and keeps new stakeholders as well as the seasoned pros on track. Author Andrew Zolli defines resilience as upholding "…core purpose and integrity among unforeseen shocks and surprises."

One of the most powerful Core Storylines was Microsoft's original mantra "A computer on every desk." Out of that came a software empire that fulfilled successfully it's own vision. The world today would be different if they'd starting writing code first and then figured out what it was for later. Yet I see this with businesses today who've lost focus on why they're doing what they're doing. They're too close to the details and the demands of getting their product out. Ask them to articulate the product story and they'll repeat a jumble of features. They've lost their Core Storyline; they've lost their way. And no amount of clever marketing after the fact will fix that.

A business may not fully embrace their Core Storyline by getting side-tracked into meaningless verbiage and believing they've found the magical Mission Statement that will solve all their problems. To say that your business is engaged with customers is not the same as actually being engaged or even striving to be engaged.

Sometimes, a strong Core Storyline needs to be abandoned and replaced. Walmart's "Low Price Leader," which drives manufacturing, supply chain, and marketing positioning, is no longer the powerful Core Storyline it once was because under the pressure of the internet, every retailer's prices are low –or low enough. In the current consumer environment of low price normalcy, shoppers want quality, service, and knowledge. With a cheap products focus, Walmart has painted itself into a corner.

Enter Lowe's with the new Core Storyline of "Never Stop Improving" which is an aspirational narrative backed by tangible products and knowledgeable in-store help. Lowe's

Core Storyline resonates with consumers, employees, and stock-holders because it aligns with tangible actions.

Job seekers fall into the trap of a weak or non-existent Core Storyline. From cover letters to coffee catch-ups to interviews, many do nothing more than repeat the details of a resume or fumble through an Elevator Speech. Most job seekers make the mistake of concentrating only on the facts of their career rather than building out stories that engage and stimulate action. Hiring officers are not machines and treating them as such will waste their time and as well as the applicant's. For job seekers, the Core Storyline helps to look forward aspirationally as opposed to looking backwards factually with a resume i.e. "This is what I've done so I'm here to do the same."

The real strength of the Core Storyline is the desire to make the world a better place. A project manager lives to organize because everyone is happier. A small business owner takes pride in putting food on her employees' table. A technical writer connects subject matter experts with readers to increase understanding; her Core Storyline is three simple words, "I translate geek."

Madeline Stuart is a vivacious, attractive, and photogenic teenager who's working as a professional model. She loves the camera and the camera loves her. Has she dedicated herself to her profession for the money? The attention? The clothes? Before I answer, there's one more thing to know about Madeline; she has Downs Syndrome. In fact, she is the first professional model with Downs. Instead of hiding away from who she is, Madeline Stuart embraces her own self and boldly shouts to the world her Core Storyline: "I hope through modelling I can change societies' view of people with disabilities."

madelinestuartmodel.com

Who's cooler than that?

I can't over-emphasize how important the Core Storyline is regardless of whether your product is a physical object, an idea, or yourself. Like our sun guides the planets' orbits, the Core Storyline exerts gravitational pull on communication efforts and business decisions.

It's not easy to find your Core Storyline and success can take many attempts; it's an ongoing process. But I challenge you to put in the effort because it's essential to your success. What's your Core Storyline?

The Credibility Storyline

Today's audience receives an overwhelming deluge of marketing messages every day that contain truth, falsehoods, or outright lies. Their brains are in a constant state of evaluation of what is real and what isn't. The Credibility Storyline is an honest report of what the product is, how it

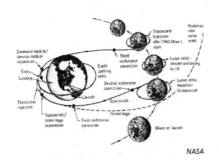

NASA

works, its usefulness, and the authority standing behind. The purpose is to open the audience to your message. In the race to the moon, the Credibility Storyline is the how of the what and the who:

"We're going to the moon using a relay series of rockets, space capsules, and lunar landers; it's a system designed by the great rocket scientist Dr. Werner Von Braun."

The Credibility Storyline establishes expert knowledge and understanding in an intelligent way. If NASA had said "We're going to the moon in a cardboard box decorated with colorful crayon drawings by Cindy," they may not have received the necessary funding from Congress.

Sean Locke --Shutterstock

The Credibility Storyline can
be straightforward. For instance,
"Homemakers swear by this
wooden spring clip that holds
cloth firmly to a cord. We call it a

Pixabay.com

clothespin." On the other hand, it doesn't have to be drab
and unentertaining. For example, *Bounty Paper Towels: The
quicker picker-upper!*® that's served well for over 40 years.
The Credibility Storyline just needs to show that the product
is real by using to-the-point messaging that demonstrates
value.

Some marketers confuse the Credibility Storyline, which
describes the product in a robust overview, with the Data
Storyline, (coming up later), which lists all the technical
specifications and details. The temptation is to "prove the
product" by pounding an endless list of features into the
listener's brain. The focus should be on what the product
does rather than the bells and whistles. McDonald's touts the
Secret Sauce that makes their burgers delicious but never
mentions the ingredients, (mayonnaise, sweet pickle relish,
yellow mustard, vinegar, garlic powder, onion powder, and
paprika), which is relegated to the Data Storyline.

At this point, your goal is to set a common context so that
your customers will know the general category while you're
establishing expert bona fides. The Credibility Storyline
describes what the product is, what it does better than its
competitors, and how it fits into the general category. It
gives the logical brain just enough facts to reassure rather
than asking it to make judgements. The Credibility Storyline
introduces benefits but steers away from features.

The Credibility Storyline can also take a well-known commodity and leverage itself into new markets. Dawn Dish Soap has launched the *Beyond the Sink* effort to change customer perception by reminding us that in addition to washing dishes well, it cleans oil off of birds and is gentle enough to use on eyeglasses. Did you know that you can slather a drop onto a wood screw to make it turn easier? Dawn is expanding its market share from dish soap to an all-around cleaner because of an established credible reputation.

The Credibility Storyline frequently employs impartial authorities to lend credence to claims. A doctor's endorsement of toothpaste, an institute's seal of approval on a kitchen blender, or a customer testimonial of a weight-loss product increases trust in a product and reassures consumers in their decisions.

Wikipedia Commons

If your product is yourself, the Credibility Storyline establishes professional status by expertise, values and achievements. Although credibility is frequently established with educational degrees and awards, real-world experience can be more effective. Anna Liotta teaches cross-generational communication and begins every presentation with "I'm the youngest girl in a family of 19." In that simple statement, she's established her expertise by the life she's lived. (If pressed, she'll also mention her Master's degree in Interpersonal Communications). In either case, one cannot doubt that the ability to communicate across generations is

Anna's special ability. We all have credibility as an expert whether in a traditional or non-traditional sense.

For a job seeker, the Credibility Storyline demonstrates to the Hiring Officer an understanding of the current business, where the applicant fits in, how they will bring value and most importantly, how the company will benefit. The candidate is the product they need.

The Experiential Storyline

The customer's experience when using the product is at the heart of the Experiential Storyline. It isn't what the product does, it's not a feature, but rather the action that a customer takes, their participation, with the product that evokes a pleasant and satisfying experience. NASA made a decision early on to open the process of space travel to the public through live TV coverage, science films for students, and profiles of the astronauts. The Experiential Storyline drew the American public into the adventure: *We're all going to the moon!*

Physical actions by the customer can trigger feelings and reasons to care about your product. Consider the emotional component: what will your customer feel? Curiosity? Excitement? Reassurance? Memories? Think about the physical senses, what will your customer see, touch, smell, or hear? Prompt the senses and imagination.

Pixabay.com

Mrs. Fields doesn't sell cookies. Whenever I pass by the bakery, the aroma of baking cookies tickles my nose and triggers emotional memories of comfort, home, and the happiness of my childhood. Without making a conscious decision, I'll open my wallet and anticipate the warm chewiness of chocolate chip on my tongue and the flow of cold milk down my throat; the aroma of fresh-baked chocolate-chip cookies is a return to innocent childhood pleasures. A Mrs. Fields cookie never disappoints. Mrs. Fields doesn't sell cookies; she sells memories.

The Experiential Storyline of Mrs. Fields zig-zags from physical to emotional. It's an experience while doing.

In the late 1950's, sales of packaged cake mixes were flat. Ernest Dichter wanted to know why so he asked customers. Homemakers told him that the simplicity of the mixes made them feel self-indulgent. Because there wasn't enough work involved, they couldn't honestly take credit at the dinner table. He suggested changing the recipe that required the

Brad Cochrane

cook to add a fresh egg. The homemaker could now claim a contribution, a sense of it pride in the cake being homemade, an Experiential Storyline of experience while doing. Sales shot up.

Food is more than nourishment; eating is an Experiential Storyline which arouses the senses of sight, smell, and taste as well as hearing in the case of a sizzling steak or the Snap-Crackle-Pop of a breakfast cereal. Curiosity, anticipation, and reward is the Experiential Storyline of a fortune cookie.

Many people enjoy drinking Ramune, a delicious soda from Asia. It's sold in a unique hourglass shaped bottle that's sealed using a clear marble inside the bottle. To open the drink, the customer has to follow an attached six-step instruction set to pop the marble loose. It takes attention, patience and skill.

In this age of consumer convenience, making the customers work to get the product seems counter-intuitive. Yet Ramune is more popular than ever. Ramune has a great Experiential Storyline because the product *is* the story. The customer makes the Ramune story a personal experience, perhaps a rite of passage for a child and a cherished memory for an adult. Remove the bottle story and Ramune is nothing more than carbonated sugar water.

Wikipedia Commons

http://www.wikihow.com/Open-and-Drink-a-Bottle-of-Ramune-Pop

Games are products that are stories. The Experiential Storyline is essential, that is, the experience while doing. The dice must be rolled, the wheels spun, and the finish line crossed. Depending on which way chance points, we win or lose, succeed or fail, celebrate or commiserate.

A demonstration of a product that puts the customer in the center of the experience is very compelling as it triggers the aspirational brain with an imaginative story of the future. Late night infomercials featuring toned athletes and sleek exercise machines promise strong bodies with only three simple payments.

In situations in which the buying process is complicated, creating a buying experience that walks the customer through the purchase is very useful. For instance, public speakers who also sell books during their presentations will show the audience exactly how to fill out an order form. An insurance company promises that a short step-by-step procedure on a phone call will save the customer money.

In my *Storytelling for Job Finders* seminar, I stress the Experiential Storyline. When interviewing for a new job, the storyline deftly paints a picture of the candidate as an already hired employee as well as a visceral experience of the day-to-day work life that can be expected. For example, the applicant might be a heads-down workhorse or a gregarious relationship builder; either is valid.

In the early days of my TV broadcast career, I worked as an audio technician but aspired to be a videographer. Yet my bosses refused to promote me. Then one day, in an on-air entertainment segment, I played a bumbling cameraman. For the first time, my bosses *saw* me as a videographer and a promotion soon followed. Similarly, job seekers can create an image in the Hiring Officer's mind of the applicant already "doing the job."

Julie Booze-Jervis, PMP, CPLP is a highly skilled project manager. When she enters a meeting room, she'll quietly arrange the chairs so that everyone can see each other. On a white board, she'll arrange facts in neat rows; her penmanship is flawless. Through her unconscious habits, she concretely demonstrates her Experiential Storyline and why "When I show up, team members breathe a sigh of relief because I organize everything."

The Hiring Officer wants to know what the candidate does beyond performing tasks to make the business successful. The unasked question is "Do I want to be around this person every day?" Use the Experiential Storyline to appeal to both the logical and aspirational brain.

Detailing the product works is never as powerful as involving the customer in a personal experience of using the product. Making the customer do something that leads to a reward engages them and stimulates increased sales.

The Experiential Storyline isn't what your product can do but rather what the customer experiences while using the product. Or what they experience because they've bought your product. Is it more powerful to show the inside workings of a dishwasher or a family enjoying themselves while the dishwasher operates silently in the background? I leave that answer to you.

The Journey Storyline

The Journey Storyline is about a person, a company, or a product that proves its worth with passion, determination, and capability. In a sense, this is the Hero's Journey with a set-back, struggle, perseverance, innovation, success, and lesson.

On January 27, 1967 three NASA astronauts sat in the Apollo 1 capsule atop the Saturn V rocket working through their checklist. It was a routine test, one of many. An errant spark, an explosion, and a fireball engulfed Gus Grissom, Ed White, and Roger Chaffee leaving them dead and the nation in mourning. In the terrible days after, it became clear that NASA wasn't giving up on the quest to go to the moon. The soul searches, rocket redesigns,  and missions that followed is the personal narrative of an organization shaken to its core but bravely struggling on to ultimate success: men on the moon.

NASA

Storylines about people are the most effective; people learn through someone else's experience. My insurance agent once sent me a personal, heartfelt, and genuine letter that I immediately knew to be different than the customary pitch. He related the story of a client to whom he'd sold a standard Home & Auto Policy. Then, he'd half-heartedly tried to upsell a life insurance plan. Feeling uncomfortable that he was being too *salesy*, he let his client push back and the matter was dropped. A few weeks later, his client died unexpectedly and left his wife and two kids in financial straits. My insurance agent berated himself up for not being more forceful with his client to buy what was really needed. He vowed to be a better person and made a promise to us (his current clients) not to let us down the way he let down his other client. Not a word about life insurance, not a word about setting up a sales meeting. He left it at that. You can see where this is going in term of selling more life insurance but do you see that the real result was an increase of trust?

Storylines about companies can be very powerful. Consider the famous Journey Storyline of the Johnson & Johnson Company. In 1982, an unknown person poisoned drugstore bottles of Tylenol pain medication resulting in seven deaths. Instead of treating this crime as an isolated incident, which it was, the company immediately recalled and destroyed all the Tylenol product thus incurring an immediate financial loss. Before relaunching Tylenol, the company introduced a tamper-proof cap. The Journey Storyline is that of a company suffering a set-back, struggling through to a solution, and finally attaining success. In a situation where public trust in the company could have been irretrievably damaged, Johnson & Johnson modeled the moral lesson of *doing the right thing* and increased trust in its product. Sales bounced back stronger than ever.

Every product has a Journey Storyline from inception to release. Regardless of what problem the product solves, the "backstory" personalizes a product making it more memorable to the consumer.

Post-it Notes, the ubiquitous yellow paper that easily sticks and unsticks, began as an absolute failure. 3M engineers had developed a new adhesive with a serious problem: the glue didn't stay stuck. With failure facing them in the face, they redefined the goal from a *permanent* adhesive to a *temporary* adhesive. On a whim, they slathered it on scrap paper –which just happened to be yellow –and passed out sample paper pads. One employee used them to mark the pages of his choir hymnal and the team realized they had a real product on their hands. Excited, the sales department visited office supply purchasers and were met with indifference; paper clips worked just fine. With an overstock of unsalable product, the salesforce gave them away to administrative assistants –who fell in love with the yellow stickies and demanded more. An industry was born. The Post-It Note story is the Mountain Plot with struggles, setbacks, and final success. It's the fable of the ugly duckling who becomes a beautiful swan. The plucky little product becomes the default choice of consumers.

The over-used phrase of *New and Improved*, alludes to an ongoing journey from good to better. Interestingly enough, as consumers, we don't see the previous versions as failures. Products celebrate progress.

The Subaru Automobile Company ran a TV commercial that begins with the aftermath of a horrible car accident. A highway patrol officer and tow truck driver are looking at the wreck. The officer simply says, "They lived." The next scene shows the smashed vehicle at the salvage yard. A wide-eyed yardman tells a co-worker, "They lived." The final scene shows a happy family coming out of their front door and the father pauses a moment to gaze upon a new Subaru and says. "We lived." Subaru's Journey Storyline "We never stop improving safety because lives matter" is vividly expressed. (https://www.youtube.com/watch?v=-oZcnH6uhLw) At a corporate level, the Journey Storyline connects to Subaru's Mission Statement:

> The mission statement for Subaru of America is a Corporate Philosophy focused on advanced technology, harmony in relationships, and global progress for the future.

For entrepreneurs, the Journey Storyline is essential in an investor pitch as a way to demonstrate passion, perseverance, and a willingness to learn from mistakes. Investors want to know that entrepreneurs in it for the long haul. Angie Hicks went door-to-door signing up subscribers for a service that rated general contractors. Investors loved Angie's demonstration of character and her company Angie's List received an influx of money and grew rapidly.

For job seekers, a Journey Storyline reveals their reaction when things go sideways. Hiring Officers want to know that candidates can recognize problems, find solutions, and implement success. A Journey Storyline is about the real person.

The Journey Storyline takes courage to tell because the natural inclination is to shy away from personal failures. Ironically, it's the very mistakes made that lead people to trust more, not because of the screw-ups but because of the lessons learned and problems overcome. Honest storytelling takes boldness and bravery but is worth the effort.

The Data Storyline

Some people use statistics like a drunk uses a lamppost,
to support but not illuminate.

-Andrew Lang

The hard facts that support claims and the features that make the product special is the Data Storyline.

Marketers often make the mistake of leading with the Data Storyline (thus triggering the logical brain that sorts quickly to a *no*). Although story comes first, remember that at times you will be communicating with the logical part of the brain. Your supporting facts need to be true, provable, and stated clearly. Statements should be layered with summaries at the top and supporting data underneath.

In some ways, the Data Storyline is like a police procedural in which the facts take precedence. It may be appropriate to list numbers in a table if for no other reason than to prove that you have your data in order. Put reference data into a reference section. Resist information overload and embrace data sharpening.

Whenever possible, give insights, not data. The characters of the Data Storyline are numbers and facts but a recitation of figures should also have personality. Link numbers to people. As Jerome Baker notes, "A fact wrapped in a story is 22 times more memorable than a pronouncement of fact."

By comparing two methods of measurement and judging if the overall statement is true, the logical brain is challenged and engaged. To paraphrase NASA, "At 363 feet, the Saturn V rocket is taller than the Statue of Liberty and more powerful than 85 Hoover Dams."

HEIGHT = 363 FT.
APOLLO / SATURN V
SPACE VEHICLE

HEIGHT = 305 FT.
STATUE OF
LIBERTY

MSFC 67 PA 187

NASA

Numbers are not just numbers; they can be given personality by adding attributes that make new connections in the brain. As mentioned earlier, the number 88 by itself has no meaning other than it comes after 87. However, with the facts that there are 88 keys on a piano, the most popular FM frequency for jazz stations is 88, and *Rocket 88* is considered the first rock and roll song, then the number 88 takes on a musical meaning. Transforming numbers into characters makes them memorable.

In technical communications, processes are described sequentially i.e. "Step 52: Insert Pin E into Hole 7." For non-detail oriented readers, instructions can be excruciating. However, if storytelling is incorporated, readers will pay closer attention because a positive (or negative) outcome is at stake. For instance, a manual for assembling a barbeque grill will garner closer attention if it begins with an image of a happy chef cooking on the grill. Or conversely, an image of an explosion. The customer imagines an outcome dependent on following –or not following– instructions. Author Jack London's short story *To Build a Fire* describes a character lost in the frozen Arctic who can only stay alive by starting a campfire. At the same time as the story of human survival transfixes the reader, the essential mechanics of building a fire is learned.

Stories will help convince listeners that they should push through technical details. Speaker Lisa Copeland begins her talk with a personal story of running a triathlon. As she describes her leg pains of Hour 14, she takes a pause and launches into the learning component. Psychologically, her audience believes that in order to hear the rest of the story, they need to pay rapt attention to the technical lessons. Near the end, Lisa wraps up her story and ties it together with the lesson. By the way, the story must relate to the lesson. If it's just an unrelated story, the audience will feel cheated.

Data stories need not be complicated either. Sometimes, a single piece of data tells the whole story. In 1895, Ivory Soap wanted to differentiate itself from competitor Castile Soap. Independent testing revealed that Ivory was purer than Castile. The slogan *Ivory is 99.44 % Pure Soap*® was born. Today, to demonstrate the reliability of the online business product Office 365, Microsoft makes a 99.9% uptime promise. A simple data fact that's important to the customer can go a long way.

Public Domain

Remember to use quantifiable measurable numbers that can be proven. With a bit of digging, you'll find statistics that startle, intrigue, and engage your customers.

Unfortunately, customers misuse data to deflect a decision. Some customers, having already decided not to buy, reconfigure the data so that logically the answer is *no*. For instance, a customer might say that the product just doesn't have enough power when in reality they hate the color. Although the salesperson might think that a discussion about facts and figures indicates a hopeful sale, it can mean the opposite. To the customer, it's polite to ask for a brochure at a trade show to end the discussion or take a business card with a promise to get in touch later. The only hope for a sale is one last effort at appealing to the aspirational brain with a story.

Some people have experienced *data bullying* in which one person recites a stream of data to intimidate another person. In business, there's an acronym for that: *IRK* or *Impressive Random Knowledge*. It's no wonder that some customers are wary of data monologues.

On the other hand, a careful review of deeper-level data can indicate that the whole data set is solid and robust. The rock band Van Halen insisted that no brown M&Ms were to be served backstage in their dressing room. Although it seems like a petulant demand by spoiled rock stars, the clause was actually put in the contract by the tour manager. Venues across the country vary in quality and competence. For example, sound and lighting for a rock show requires abundant electrical power. In too many instances, the local promoter wouldn't read the contract closely enough to realize that extra power lines had to be provided. To fix that oversight, the *no brown M&Ms* clause was buried deep inside the contract. When a tour manager came to the venue and saw brown M&Ms, he'd know that the local promoter hadn't read the contract thoroughly. He'd then proactively search out additional oversights.

If the offering is a Big Data application, the logical tendency is to explain it in terms of data. Be mindful as you'll need to prove data with data but still need to trigger the aspirational brain. Stories about Big Data tend to talk about the overall benefits for a large group of people using a statistical approach. Big Data is about insights and discovering solutions rather than the volume of data itself.

For instance, it's beneficial to a health care provider to use Big Data systems for centralizing physician notes, test results, and patient prescriptions. But the real benefit is saving the life of an individual patient. The Story First Marketing approach is to *Think Globally but Act Locally* with a personal story. Instead of trumpeting that a new prescription tracking system saves the hospital money, show that grandma gets the care she needs to stay alive.

The power of Big Data is that by integrating different classes of data into information that new insights are revealed. Big Data isn't really new but first glimmered back in the 19th Century during a dark time.

The old lady was dead, the little girl was dying and there was nothing that Dr. John Snow could do to change that. Cholera had struck London in the Year of Our Lord 1854 and the SoHo neighborhood was taking the brunt of death's icy sword. As John left the grieving family, he walked the streets convinced that there was a puzzle to be solved, a piece hidden in plain sight. As he passed the tightly packed homes and somber doors, he counted the black wreaths indicating a death in the family. On Broad Street, he glanced at the community water pump and stopped in his tracks. Could there be a single source of infection? Was that it? Yes, it had to be. The sick ones must have all drunk from this hand pump!

John went to the authorities and explained that something was wrong with the water. Nonsense, they replied. Everyone knows that cholera is the result of bad air, not water; that's a scientific fact, a certainty accepted by all the best doctors. They sent this rebellious physician on his way.

At home, Dr. Snow laid out his map of London and made marks upon it; each noted a death as well as a location and they all clustered around the Broad Street Water pump. Here was proof! Dr. John Snow took his map to the authorities and, finally understanding, they immediately removed the handle from the Broad Street pump. With the removal of the infected water the cholera epidemic was stopped in its tracks.

And what of London and Dr. Snow? With the epidemic over, people returned to SoHo, families strolled the streets, and Dr. Snow returned to work after having changed the world.

Dr. Snow's map combined two different classes of data, location of deaths and location of water supplies to create information and an insight that not only saved lives but gave birth to the scientific field of epidemiology. In a sense, Big Data owes its heritage to Dr. Snow.

John Snow via Wikipedia Commons

John Snow

Rsabbatini via Wiki Commons

The Big Data industry needs stories that illuminate how meta-data manifests itself in a personal, singular story that makes an individual's life better. It's not just data, its people's lives. Fight a natural inclination to speak in generalities and big picture jargon; Make data personal and emulate Dr. Snow, the first data warrior.

Use data in the right place and at the right time. The Data Storyline is a reference library from which to pull facts that are salient to the current conversation. When telling an aspirational story, sprinkle in a few factual details to ground the story and lend the storyteller credibility. But don't overdo it. Save the data download for the end as reassurance or even a separate reference section.

Unfortunately, at the end of the day, your customers are human –not data points.

-Carolyn Fuson

To review, your Marketing Story is a tapestry and the Five Storylines are threads woven within. Sometimes you'll use one thread, other times two or three, and sometimes all five. It depends on the tapestry you want to weave and the story you need to tell. Communicate to others the way in which they want to be communicated.

The Five Storylines for Marketers	
1	Core Storyline
2	Credibility Storyline
3	Experiential Storyline
4	Journey Storyline
5	Data Storyline

Core Storyline

Action statement. Passion and purpose that drives activities and keeps efforts focused and on track. Organizes efforts and communicates goals clearly to others.

- What:
- Why:

Credibility Storyline

Top-level view of how the product works that sets context as well as establishing professional status and credibility by acumen, expertise, values, and achievements.

Experiential Storyline

The delivered experience including what the customer does and their resulting emotional state.

- Customer experience
- How they feel

Journey Storyline

Demonstrates passion, perseverance and capability.

- Goal
- Surprise
- Set-back
- Struggle
- Insight
- Success
- Lesson Learned

Data Storyline

Hard facts that support claims and prove worth.

- Resume, CV, LinkedIn, etc.

What are your Five Storylines and how will you tell them?

Creating Stories

Five Steps to Story

We live in a media-saturated world in which entertainment trumps information, story trumps data. More than ever before, marketers are asked to find stories within their own industry and organizations. Our culture is hungry for facts but wants to be told in the form of a story or Narrative Non-Fiction, that is, a documentary about your own product, business, or idea.

With years in the broadcast documentary industry for such shows as *Frontline*, *Dateline*, *Biography*, and more, I've learned to look for the underlying truth of a subject and tell that truth in a matter that is genuine and credible. To that end, producers use a process to get from idea to finished production. First, we set a goal by developing a hypothesis which becomes the organizing principle around which our work is organized. Then the subject is investigated by reviewing the available material and generating primary content through interviews. Next, we evaluate our research and interviews and make a comparison to the hypothesis established at the beginning. Then we start the creative process of writing and rewriting, editing ruthlessly and without pity until a complete, vibrant, and insightful documentary emerges. In a final step, we release our story to the world and publicize as well as defend it.

I've put the process of documentary Narrative Non-Fiction into the Five Steps to Story.

1. **Set a Goal**
2. **Investigate**
3. **Evaluate**
4. **Create**
5. **Release**

Along the way, I'll show you the best way to gather authentic stories, organize your material, and champion your message.

Step 1 –Set a Goal

If you don't know where you're going, you'll end up someplace else.

-*Yogi Berra*

In pre-historic times, cave paintings were used as a tool to plan future hunts. Through the picture story, a young hunter learned what to do in the task ahead: "Hunt ibex with a bow and arrow while sneaking up behind from downwind." In

Lascaux Caves

the self-empowerment community it's called visioning, in business it's codified as project management, in technical communications it's called help documentation, and in the scientific discipline it's defined as a hypothesis: an educated guess that's proven right or wrong through rigorous testing. I call it creating a *Best Case Scenario* that sets a clear goal and outcome. The rationale behind this approach is to organize efforts, allocate resources, and energize actions.

Set a goal using an approach that's most comfortable to you. Some people chart out whiteboard diagrams, others design detailed workbooks, and some souls make collages that hang over their work area. The best technique is to use the one that works for you and that you will work.

If the spreadsheet had been developed back then, the cave painting might have looked like this framework:

E1		

▲	A	B
1	**What are we hunting?**	Ibex
2	**Why?**	Survive Feast
3	**Who?**	Old Hunters Young Hunters
4	**Tools?**	Bow & Arrow Our wits
5	**Strategy**	Sneak up behind Kill at a distance
6	**Story: Context**	We need food so must hunt
7	**Story: Complication**	Ibex are hard to kill so we must learn how
8	**Story: Result**	Success We eat!
9	**Summary Statement**	Hunt ibex with a bow and arrow while sneaking up behind down wind
10		
11		

Sheet1 ⊕

Your first task is to create a clear goal around which to develop your story; pick a direction and destination to make your journey that much easier. Remember Billy Mills and his Gold Medal race at the Olympics? He generated a clear and precise Best Case Scenario: winning the 10,000 Meter race at the 1964 Olympics. A vague goal will not get you where you need to be.

When watching television news or documentaries, a common misconception of the audience is that a producer researches all available material, interviews subjects in meticulous depth, carefully sifts and sorts, and finally produces a story that's comprehensive and complete. If that were the case, a documentary would never make it to your television set. Broadcasting every fact, interview, and picture would be a stream of images without context, direction, or insight. By necessity, the only way to make sense of material is to pick a point-of-view ahead of time. Then it's a matter of sorting what's relevant and what's not. Can the perspective change? Absolutely and it frequently does. Frequently, that point-of-view will transform as we vigorously scrutinize our assumptions and seek robust truths. For the lucky, a nugget of gold is discovered that changes the perspective and takes the documentary towards a new and better destination.

Describe your Best Case Scenario as fully as possible. You'd be surprised how many people skip over the basics and then regret it later. Use as many nouns, adjectives, and verbs as possible to make it robust, full, and complete.

The Four Steps to the Best Case Scenario

Step 1

List simple quantitative information

Quantitative

Product X

(Marketing Message)

Call to Action

(Try)

(Buy)

(Tell)

Customer Concern

(Solve problem)

(Save money)

(Other)

Customer

(Role)

(Environment)

Product

(Definition)

(Purpose)

(Features)

(Traits)

Strategy

(Brand)

(Positioning)

Step 2

Add qualitative attributes around the audience's emotion and perception

Qualitative

Emotion

(Inspiration)

(Trust)

(Need)

(Confidence)

(Other)

Step 3

Develop the Story

Story

Structure

(Struggle)

(Setback)

(Success)

If a movie, it would be a _____

The lesson learned is_____

Step 4

Edit all notes into a Summary Statement.

Summary Statement

Lorem ipsum dolor sit amet, consectetuer adipiscing elit. Maecenas porttitor congue massa.

For instance, say that you're marketing a mobile phone application that brings together people for romance. The launch date is coming up soon so you decide to interview early testers about their experience. The Four Steps to the Best Case Scenario might look like this:

Step 1

Quantitative

> **Product**: True Love App
>> **Strategy**: Find love now!
>
> **Call to Action**
>> Buy the App
>
> **Customer Concern**
>> Find a romantic partner
>
> **Customer**
>> Lonely person
>
> **Product**
>> This simple phone application connects people who are looking for a romantic relationship
>
> **Strategy**
>> Best technology for real people

Step 2

Qualitative

> **Emotion**
>> Customer should feel that they trust the app, optimistic that they can find romance, and inspired to take the next step.

Step 3

Structure

> People looking for romance waste time using a hit or miss approach. They end up dating the wrong person or, worse, just miss meeting the right person. The True Love App connects people to the right partner faster.

If a movie, it would be a romantic comedy.

The lesson learned is that sometimes true love needs a helping hand.

Step 4

The Best Case Scenario for the Find True Love App *is an adventure comedy in which a boy just misses, through a series of humorous missteps, meeting the right girl until the* Find True Love App *brings them together for happily ever after. Sometimes, true love needs a helping hand.*

With the Best Case Scenario's Summary Statement in hand, you can confidently go in the right direction as you build your Narrative Non-Fiction story with real-world personal experiences, insights, and lessons learned along the way, that is, the moral to the story: *Sometimes, true love needs a helping hand.*

The Best Case Scenario has four major points: The Setting, The Problem, The Solution, and The Lesson (which mirrors the Story Structure of Context, Complication, Result, and Lesson). Add attributes that clarify and embellish the story. Specify the type: adventure, mystery, comedy, drama, or something else. Consider the tone: factual or emotional, serious or light, a point-of-view that is removed, or personal. Make your product essential to the story, the problem can't be solved without your product. The clearer your vision, the better your result.

Step 2 –Investigate

If you want the answer –ask the question.

-Lorii Myers

With digital resources, researching a product is easier than ever. But treat any information you find online with skepticism and always double-check facts; an oft-repeated lie is no less false. Use different types of sources to cast a wider net such as news articles, books, journals, archived company and product material, and internal marketing strategies. Think globally but look locally; ask around as insights may come from a friend of a friend. Immerse yourself in the

Pixabay.com

product and find previous customer stories. Reference librarians are some of the smartest people in the world and a visit to the local library can yield unexpected results. Don't overlook university libraries, business libraries, and company libraries. Visit the production line or manufacturing facilities. Strike up a conversation with the people doing the work. Seek out authoritative sources such as experts in the field, university professors, and researchers. Create your own primary content through formal interviews.

For job seekers, request an informational interview with someone in an industry, company, or group in which you're interested. Without the pressure of an actual job interview, people love to talk about themselves and their work. Frequently, they may know of an available position.

Know your product cold. What does it do? Where did it come from; how was it created? Where's it made? Sold? You need to know everything there is to know. Next, look beyond the obvious. What does your product or service do besides solving an obvious problem? What's the real benefit?

Here's an interesting fact: Over 100 years ago no one had bad breath. It's true. But a quiet little chemical company in St. Louis was manufacturing a disinfectant cleaning solution for medical examining rooms; it was a nice little niche market that was dependable if unspectacular. Then one day, they looked at their product in a different manner and realized that in the same way their chemical compound killed germs on a surface it would kill germs in a mouth. Some of those little critters gave off a pungent smell. Listerine quickly invented *Halitosis* and with it the

Public Domain

billion-dollar mouthwash industry. The marketing approach introduced the story of a young woman who was never asked to marry –an important cultural norm in those days –because her bad breath made her unattractive to suiters. Then she discovered that Listerine freshened her breath and multiple proposals followed. With the addition of an emotional story

—fresh breath insures romantic happiness —a chemical commodity became a sought-out specialty product.

In the research process, you'll collect more material than you'll ever need; it's easy to get lost in the content. It's never too early to organize a coherent system so that you can find relevant information later. In whichever way you organize, be consistent. An excellent system for keeping track is by marking each piece of content as it comes in with a control number. Enter the control number into a master list along with a short description and location. This approach will help you quickly find specific content later.

#	Description	Type	Location
01	MyProduct Brochure 2010	Paper	File Box
02	White Paper Sales Strategy	Digital	Desktop>MyProduct>01_Wht_Papr
03	Customer Reviews	Online	www.myproduct.com/cust_rev
04			
05			
06			

You'll need a file box, manila folders, marking pen, a loose-leaf notebook, and a computer. First, create a Master List similar to the previous as a table or a spreadsheet. For paper material, mark the first page, insert into a manila folder (similarly marked), and store in a file box. For a downloaded digital file, rename the file beginning with the control number and then the title. For online resources, you'll need to copy URL. Use the loose-leaf notebook to gather top-level material such as your Master List, contact information, calendars, and top-level ideas.

As you research, organize the top-level ideas in a coherent arrangement that becomes the basis for your story.

Whichever configuration you choose, use the Best Case Scenario as a guide. I usually write it out *in pencil* in a prominent place. Occasionally in your research, you'll find a note that doesn't ring true, an assumption in the Best Case Scenario that is flat out wrong. Some writers will try to change the facts to fit the Best Case Scenario but the better approach is to change the Best Case Scenario to fit the facts. A skeptical customer will see right through a story that isn't true and embrace a story that is. The Best Case Scenario is a guideline written in sand and not a law chiseled in stone.

The News Approach or the 5 "W's" and "H" is a very popular method for organizing top-level ideas that asks the questions of Who, What, Where, When, Why, and How. It's excellent for collecting facts and straightforward reporting but can lack depth, a larger context, and the narrative storytelling structure.

News Approach
Who
What
Where
When
Why
How

The Hierarchical Outline is the classic method of organizing. Beginning with the top-level theme, ideas are added as sub-themes. Although it lacks some freedom and creativity, it's a common method that's been mastered by most people.

1. Theme
   a. Sub Theme A
   b. Sub Theme B
      i. Idea
      ii. Idea

Mind Mapping is my personal favorite as I can collect top-level information in an organic approach. From a central hub idea, topic spokes extend outward as facts are added to expanding shafts. Confined to a single page, it's a great way to have an overall look at the material.

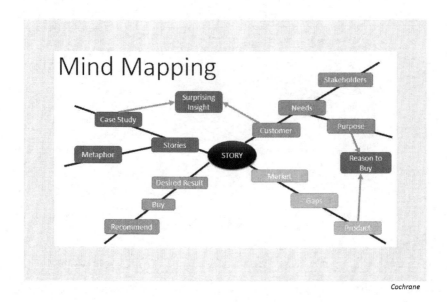

Cochrane

If you're a business marketer, creating stories about your customers, company and product is part of the job. That means that you'll need to interview people –which sounds a lot easier than it actually is. I've interviewed thousands of real people drawing out their real stories using techniques that elicit stories that are interesting, genuine, and powerful.

Remember that you're in the business of Narrative Non-Fiction. Look at your efforts as if you are making a documentary about your own product, business or idea – because you are. To find true stories, start with a plan but be open to chance and opportunity. Open your ears and eyes and tell everyone that you're looking for stories; embrace all sources. The "best" employee may not be the best for your story; the strongest story may come from an oft-overlooked worker. Look for people that represent your Best Case Scenario.

On a Hawaiian beach, TV Producer Victoria Lewin and her neighborhood friends watched the sun go down. It was a casual community gathering complete with beer, a bonfire, and easy conversation –a time for stories. A neighbor related the journey of the family Taiko drum from Japan to this particular island in the vast Pacific. Victoria felt drawn in as she realized that this was a personal tale of a family and a culture emigrating to a new homeland. In the unlikeliest of places, Victoria had found a powerful story that consumed the next year of her life. *Great Grandfather's Drum* is an award-winning television documentary that's recognized as a definitive expression of the Japanese culture in Hawaii.

Although it's best to conduct interviews without pre-judging, the Best Case Scenario can keep you from following tangents (as interesting as they may be). Having been involved in several Emmy winning documentaries over the years, I know just how important the original point-of-view is to drive the day-to-day work forward. If you decide that you'd rather just collect what comes along, then you aren't making a documentary film but surveillance tapes.

That said, the point-of-view in Narrative Non-Fiction can change, and frequently does, as serendipity takes over and pre-conceived misconceptions are put to rest. A good documentary team is always open to revelation and insight, the undiscovered nuggets waiting to be picked up.

I'm very proud of photographing the PBS documentary *Those People*. In the early days of the AIDS/HIV epidemic, sufferers were marginalized by many mainstream Americans who were unsympathetic to their plight. Producer Georgia Smith set out to change that perception and show patients as real people with hopes, dreams, and challenges just like anyone else. During a routine interview with a young man named Shaun, who was listing his daily medication intake, we were interrupted by a knock on the door. Shaun's mother had stopped by to check up on him and so we suggested that she join the interview. What followed was a mother's expression of sadness, love, and acceptance that illustrated more than any fact or figure that AIDS/HIV had a human toll on real people. Mother and son touched the audience changing those who watched as well as the social conversation.

Interviewing a customer is different than interviewing an employee. A customer will tend to talk about success and bypass the challenges. An employee will be careful not to offend management. Dig into their business and environment. What are the real gaps? Who are the real stakeholders? An understanding of their personal motivation will help you get to the valuable stories that are about overcoming real problems.

Grainger is a company that supplies industry with the basics of building maintenance. Business was flat, not losing share but not really gaining much either. By interviewing customers, they found out that the typical purchase was a one-off purchase from a local store; employees bought one item at a time. Think about how expensive this approach is when factoring in worker time spent finding, purchasing, and accounting for a simple mop. With this insight, Grainger provided an online one-stop shop and offered to take over companies internal purchasing and processing while absorbing overhead costs themselves. Companies saved money and Grainger increased market share –a win-win for all. It's no wonder that Grainger's slogan is *For the ones who get it done*®.

As you interview employees, encourage them to describe their insight and epiphany moment. How did they act on it? Were they discouraged? How did they prevail?

Interviewing is more than asking a few questions; it's a guided conversation that establishes a personal connection to gather facts, insights, and lessons. I've learned, sometimes the hard way, these important points:

- *Prepare, share, and listen.*
- *Your questions aren't as important as their answers.*

First, **prepare**. Research your interviewee's role, background, and personal interests. Plan out the conversation, topics, and touchpoints. Don't waste people's time.

Next, **share**. Start the interview by sharing something about yourself. Then ask an easily answered factual question, such as name and spelling, to get the conversation rolling. This is a great way to put the interviewee at ease and talking while establishing a personal connection. Beginning with a gentle "what" helps move into the harder "why" later. Always be respectful to build trust. Peppering rapid-fire questions puts people on the defensive and results in short terse unhelpful answers.

More often than you'd like, you'll encounter an unpleasant interviewee. No matter how objectionable that person may be, decide that on some level there is something to like about them. You may not agree with their words but there is something good to find in nearly everybody so use that as a way to build rapport. For a TV news story, I once interviewed an avowed racist in his home. Although he represented a group that I abhor and he said truly hateful things, I complimented him on the landscaping of his yard of which he was justifiably proud. With that shred of friendliness, he opened up and I let his own words condemn himself.

Then, **listen**. Really listen. It's a conversation, not an interrogation. Model relaxed and open behavior. Draw out stories with open-ended questions but keep the conversation on track. Dig for personal experiences and lessons. Listen for what motivates them, their passion. The best answers are stories that relate a failure, a struggle, and success.

Sometimes in a conversation, people like to engage in back and forth argument. Asking a question that the interviewee can argue against can bring forth an answer that is cogent and heartfelt. A word of caution; it's a technique that should be used judiciously and respectfully.

Remember that their answers are more important than your questions. Spend less time preparing a list of questions and more time preparing the topics to explore. During the interview, don't move onto the next question before obtaining a satisfactory answer. Or make a note to come back to the topic later. And don't interrupt the flow of conversation with questions that are long or confusing; your job is to guide the discussion.

I once hid behind a fake wall for a hidden-camera TV commercial. For legal reasons, the subjects had to be unaware of the cameras yet needed to say the correct marketing message. Our interviewer couldn't simply ask, "We're shooting a commercial so please say Scope mouthwash is great." He presented himself as a not too bright guy who was hard of hearing. During the interview, he kept re-asking questions and clarifying answers by pretending he missed what they said. In frustration, the subjects would eventually give the correct answer delivered with energy: "Scope with T-2-5 makes my mouth minty fresh!" *(https://www.youtube.com/watch?v=QVbWD0R1CPY)* The answers are more important than the questions.

Conducting on-camera video interviews takes skill, practice, and intention. Making a video is much more than pressing a button. Great interviewing is paying attention in the moment, guiding the energy of your subject, and mastering an innate sense of how simple words become a complex story. In video production, always use professionals as you can't cheap your way to the top.

Think about the kind of answers you're getting and why. Is your subject giving stock answers, protecting themselves, or getting off track and deep-diving on irrelevant points? You need to control the interview by modeling open-ended conversation, guide them back to the subject, and clarify answers. Above all, you need to be on their side.

Stone59 via Wikipedia Commons

During an interview, some people will get nervous and develop a lack of confidence in themselves and their answers. It can happen to anyone and your response needs to be supportive and kind. I once interviewed guitar virtuoso Carlos Santana for the American Music Awards on ABC-TV. The poor guy tripped into the well of self-consciousness and doubt. Think about that. Carlos Santana. *The* Santana. The best of the best could barely utter a full coherent sentence. What did I do? Go over the questions until he got it right? Pressure his performance? No. I stopped the recording and we chatted about the weather. The *weather!* Of all things, I talked to my childhood musical hero about California mudslides. But it worked because we connected, built rapport, and established trust. I started recording again and we had a wonderful relaxed conversation that was full of succinct, powerful, and memorable sound-bites that entertained a national television audience.

Beware of the yarn which is an amusing anecdote but has nothing to do with your Best Case Scenario. Perhaps it's a tale that rambles with no point in sight and no lesson learned. Often, people tend to delve into details, over-correcting and over-verbalizing their answers. Guide interviewees back on track by asking for clarification around the important themes. It's OK to interrupt anecdotes (but never rudely) and move the conversation forward.

Just as a story has a complication, it also needs a tangible result or it's not really a story. In life, complications don't always have results. To check that you're hearing an actual story, look for the result first and then backtrack to the complication. Complications must be significant to the human condition such as fear, love, pain, death, or hate. There should be a risk that's personalized (a rich person losing a car has a different "risk" than a poor person) and look for motivation, that is, the underlying emotional conviction of *why* someone did what they did. For instance, you may find a story about the company's production line breaking down and then rebuilt to be more efficient than before the failure. However, told from an employee perspective, the problem of a production-line failure threatens the company's viability and a real risk to a job, food, and shelter –tough times. So the real story is the employee working late into the night to solve the problem and ensuring the survival of their family. Look for stories that have a satisfying ending, where everything works out in a positive way.

During the interview, listen for common problems, authenticity and passion, unexpectedness, new approaches, personal growth, lessons learned, and a moral to the story all in the context of struggles, setbacks, success, and completion. Find that something extra with relatable characters and an engaging hook.

For my interviews, I use The Conversation Map as an organizational tool to record important details, keep the discussion on track, and highlight the essential elements of a great story as well as having the flexibility to circle back to important points without missing a thing. The questions don't have to be asked in order as long as all the story elements are covered in the end. It reminds

Public Domain

me to ask open-ended questions and collect answers as stories.

As a general approach,

1. Start with the Familiar
2. Ask about a Surprise
3. Probe for a Set-Back
4. Listen for a Struggle
5. Celebrate a Success
6. Dig for the Lesson Learned

The Conversation Map

Best Case Scenario Summary Statement:

Structure	Eliciting Questions	Answers as a story
Familiar	Tell me about yourself.	*Name, Positon, Job*
Surprise	Tell me about a situation that happened...	
	What surprised you?	
Set-Back	Tell be about a setback.	
Struggle	Tell me about a struggle	
	How did you overcome it?	
Success	What did success look like?	
Lesson Learned	What did you learn?	
	Why was the product essential to the story?	*Product X made this possible because...*

Download The Conversation Map at www.Story1stMarketing.com

1. Copy the Best Case Scenario into the Summary box to stay on track. For instance, *the* Find True Love App *is an adventure comedy in which a boy just misses, through a series of humorous missteps, meeting the right girl until the* Find True Love App *brings them together for happily ever after. Sometimes, true love needs a helping hand.*

2. Begin with the Familiar and gather facts about the person, company, and product for later reference.
3. Then ask about a surprising thing, something unexpected that happened in their business or personal life. (Sometimes personal history is a great metaphor for business life).
4. Next, ask about a set-back. People want to paint a picture that everything is perfect but everyone faces obstacles. Let your interviewee know its OK to talk about difficulties because dilemmas are a universal human experience.
5. Now that the problem has been established, ask about the struggle that ensued. What were the frustrations, roadblocks? In addition to what occurred, dig for emotional descriptions like "I was lost in a fog and couldn't see my way clearly."
6. Struggles lead to success. Ask how the problem was solved using the product. Get an overview as well as revealing details and insights. Resolutions must be satisfying and solve the specific complication. What is the real resolution? Dig into the unobvious. (Is it winning a certificate of appreciation or is it that you taught one kid to read?)
7. Finally, find the conclusion and personal lesson that was learned thanks to the product.

With some luck, you'll have a personal story like this:

Even though I was desperately lonely, I thought 'Why waste money on an app?' Then I took a chance and found Cathy at the next table over. Without the Find True Love App, *I'd still be having coffee by myself*

Step 3 –Evaluate

By now, you should have one or more great stories. If not, go back for more research because a suitable story is waiting for you. Once you have a solid story, compare and test that to the Best Case Scenario.

Pixabay.com

The notion isn't to match your found story precisely to your original story but use the Best Case Scenario as a guide to confirm that you've hit all your major points as well as double-checking that you haven't strayed too far from your initial idea.

Does your story match the Best Case Scenario goals, tools, and strategy? Does your story have the essential details? For instance, did you answer the 5 W's and an H? Is there a clear idea, product, or point-of-view?

Is it engaging and clearly understood? Could your story stand by itself supported by a dramatic structure with Context, Complication, and Result? Does the story complete itself in a satisfying way?

Above all, is your story genuine? Does it resonate? Your audience is highly skilled at spotting lies and make-believe so whatever narrative non-fiction story you arrive at must ring true. Solid research and honest interviews will reveal truths that are real and authentic.

The children's story *The Velveteen Rabbit* is about a children's stuffed animal toy that is so well played with that its artificial fur has rubbed off, seams are torn, and ears have frayed: it's a shabby thing that's literally been loved to pieces. But the Velveteen Rabbit, in the act of being loved, of being seen as real, magically becomes a real rabbit, an authentic live creature.

Margery Williams –Public Domain

In a similar way, authenticity needs to be poked, squeezed, and bounced around. The bright shiny surface needs to be worn off to reveal what is real underneath and what isn't. Then and only then will your story be deemed worthwhile.

Finding authenticity isn't always easy. Facts get in the way as the logical brain takes over and recites true facts but not the truth of something. The best approach is to tap into the intuitive part of the brain and turn off logic. Your brain is smarter than you think. Quiet the ongoing internal dialogue by meditating, walking in the woods, whatever will get you out of your own head and into a receptive mood. Let words bubble up in non-organized way and be aware of how they make you feel: excited or bored? If you have conflicting stories and can't decide which is more authentic, imagine holding one in each hand. Which is lighter? Your brain is communicating to you subconsciously.

You may be rolling your metaphorical eyes about now. After all, unfettered imagination has nothing to do with scientific thinking. Or does it? When I think of Albert Einstein, I picture him scribbling formulas on a blackboard. However, the good professor liked fresh air and one beautiful day, as he sat in the sun thinking about nothing and letting his imagination run free, an image of himself riding a sunbeam popped into his head. One thing led to another and the *Theory of Relativity* was born. One of the most important scientific breakthroughs revealed itself when the logical part of Albert Einstein's brain was off-duty.

Professor Einstein often said that "Imagination is more important than knowledge." That doesn't mean that knowledge is unimportant (after all, he needed to have knowledge of higher level mathematics to translate his insight into a tangible formula) but that both imagination and knowledge need to be balanced.

An attribute of authenticity is passion, either your own or someone else's. That's not to say that passion alone makes an idea authentic but rather that humans relate to authenticity in some degree because they recognize the passion in another. If my fellow cave dweller is excited about this new thing he calls *spear* then I'll have a closer look.

Finally, does your story have action and emotion, structure and rhythm? Does it follow the model of Story First Marketing that leads with story, introduces the product, and can only be completed with your product? Ultimately, this is a judgement call. Choose your best candidate and start writing.

Step 4 –Create

Generating creative work is not for the faint of heart.
-Julien Jarreau

Writers have a saying that on a bad day they have to rewrite a piece seven times. On a good day, only six. There's no way around rewrites. Once you've found your best story, the one that matches most closely to your Best Case Scenario, write it. And rewrite it. And again. Writing is a circular process of writing and editing until an effective, memorable, relatable, robust story emerges.

Writing, editing, and proofreading are distinct processes and each employ unique skills. Write for *ideas*, edit for *structure*, and proofread for *polish*. Writing is a right brain activity that expresses ideas and creative originality. Editing and proofreading are left brain activities that dispassionately seek errors and technical perfection.

Many writers get mixed up the processes, for instance by focusing on spelling and punctuation when writing 1st drafts, and become stuck behind writer's block. Don't overthink, avoid perfectionism, and avoid the trap of Analysis Paralysis.

Writing is very personal and at the same time very public. It's an interactive process in which you'll engage other stakeholders to pick and poke at it until you get it just right. Propose, adjust, and agree. Learn the difference between critiques and criticisms; a critique is a dispassionate evaluation of the writing while a criticism is a personal judgement of the writer. Every stakeholder must agree on free expression that won't be punished. Start with what works before discussing what doesn't. Be gentle.

Earlier we looked at how an aspirational story triggers seven areas of the brain including those that process language comprehension, colors and shapes, scents, sounds, and movement. The brain knows only what comes in through its neural pathways. The senses of hearing and smell are ancient and so are more closely connected to the emotional brain. A description of a sensory experience such as a smell or sound will seem real, in some degree, to the brain. Sight is not far behind as 98% of people think in pictures; descriptions that use images are powerful. Kinesthetic, that is, physical action or even just imagining action is the most powerful way to learn. Detailed sensory descriptions trigger more parts of the brain than data and make the story real. Writers take note.

Pick a point-of-view. Cameras have specific functions that adjusts light, focus, and color. But, aside from 360 degree cameras, all cameras have one thing in common: they are used to establish a point-of-view which contains certain visual elements while excluding others. A photographer carefully chooses those elements, arranges them in a dynamic design, uses contrast and color to evoke mood, adjusts focus and sharpness to separate objects, and communicates meaning through what we see and what action is taking place. In the same way, a story informs the audience how to position their own internal mental camera.

Stories also have a tone that conveys to the listener how to interpret information. As any dog owner knows, it's not what you say to your pooch but how you say it. An academic tone implies authority while a casual tone implies friendliness. Academic writing is for the writer, marketing writing is for the reader. Depending on why your listener wants your information, you might take one tack or the other.

One way to know if you've a good solid story is to tell it in different ways. Perhaps you've chosen one perspective but later come to find that the story is better told from another perspective. For instance, are the Harry Potter books about a boy wizard who struggles and triumphs against evil? Or are they about Severus Snape, a man keeping a promise to the woman he loves to protect her son no matter the pain? The answer: both.

Lead the brain in a circle from verbs to nouns, emotion to facts, aspirations to reality, and back again. It's like arranging a song with notes, rhythm, pacing, tone, pitch, beats, and variations that pleases the ear and conveys emotion. Have your story move to make it memorable.

Think about what structure works best for your story. Is it the Hero's Journey? The Story Mountain or Plot Diagram?. The Hierarchical Outline or the News Approach?

Cochrane's Story Table is another way of organizing top-level information and builds the story as you go along. For example, the Derby the Dog story…

Cochrane's Story Table

Structure	Notes	Story
Hook	A smiling dog	Derby is happy malamute with a quick smile and even quicker wag of the tail.
Context	We love dogs	He lives with his adopted family who loves him very much.
Characters and Setting	Dog and the people who care. 3D Systems	But Derby was born with deformed front legs which means that he'll never get to run and play like other dogs. But one day, Tara Anderson met Derby and her heart opened up to this dog. She vowed to help Derby.
Complication	Dog has deformed legs; struggles	
Motivating Incident	Broken heart; someone needs to help	Derby already used a wheeled contraption for his front legs but it never worked very well.
Set Back	Wheel rig doesn't work well	It just so happened that Tara worked for 3D Systems which makes 3D printers and she brought Derby's story to the company. Everyone wanted to help and before long Derby had a new set of plastic composite legs made by the people at 3D Systems.
False Success	3D Legs	
Twist	3D Legs aren't the right size	
Resolution	3D legs in the shape of a half wheel	But unfortunately, the legs just weren't quite right. But that's the thing about 3D Printers, if the first prototype doesn't work, you can quickly redesign and make another set. Or another set.
Final Twist	Derby runs free	Well, it took three tries but today Derby has legs that let her run and play just like any other dog.
Lesson	You can change the world with 3D Systems	All thanks to a machine with skills and people with a heart at 3D Systems.

As a final check, make sure your story has the following:

✖	**Summary Checklist**
	Essential Details
	Genuine, engaging, and clearly understood
	Clear action goal of idea, feeling, or product?
	Action and Emotion
	Structure and Rhythm
	Product is essential support of the story

The needs of the reader come first. Write and rewrite your stories so they are powerful, robust, and memorable. Two stories can have the same details but one is notable and the other not. Do you know the ocean-going passenger ship the *Olympic*? Perhaps you've heard of her sister ship the *Titanic*.

Remember, stories are action and emotion. Use action to generate curiosity and as pleasant exercise for the brain. Use emotion to nudge the audience into a new perspective. Marketing stories are a journey from feeling to learning to inspiration to action. Show passion, overcome fear, and be bold!

There comes a time when you have to be done. With that, we're gonna call this painting finished.

-Bob Ross,
The Joy of Painting

Step 5 –Release

Take a deep breath: this is the moment when you release your story to the world. Congratulations; you've done it! Time to take a break and bask in a job well done.

But not quite yet… A great story needs a great storyteller and champion. That's you! Learn to express your story in any format at any time to anyone.

In addition to selling outwards to customers, you'll sell inwards and upwards to executives, employees, and stockholders because internal support is essential. Frequently, we have to get others within our organization come on board with the marketing story. To whom do you answer?

Back in the 1960's, Clairol was riding the success of their ubiquitous hair dye products. Shirley Polykoff had written the successful tagline *Does she or doesn't she? Only her hairdresser knows for sure*®. But now she was having trouble convincing her superiors that a campaign focused specifically on a blonde hair dye would be successful. Then one day, a postmarked letter arrived from a young woman:

> *My boyfriend, Harold, and I were keeping company for five years but he never wanted to set a date. This made me very nervous. I am twenty-eight and my mother kept saying soon it would be too late for me.*

The note went on to describe a Clairol advertisement that convinced her to take a chance on the blonde hair dye. Suddenly, Harold beheld his familiar girlfriend in a new light. She was so grateful to Clairol for his sudden change of heart that she wrote a thank you letter from her *honeymoon!"*

Copies of the letter were passed around the office and soon coming to the attention of the boss. Ms. Polykoff's campaign was immediately approved and the world was given *Is it true… blondes have more fun?* ®

Public Domain

Unsurprisingly, the letter became famous in advertising circles. Long after Shirley retired, she was honored at a testimonial dinner. As she stood at the podium gazing at hundreds of her fellow advertising peers, she related the story of the letter and the big impact it made on her career. "The funny thing is," she said to her breathless audience, "I wrote that letter."

To be clear, I'm not suggesting that you lie to your boss but you *do* need to believe in your story and become its best advocate. Assimilate your story so that you can tell it in any situation from Elevator Speech to Interview to Presentation.

Telling Stories

Tell it Well!

By now, you'll have a well-developed story that's engaging, powerful, and robust as well as your Five Storylines to mix, match, and weave in the right message for the right audience. Now it's time to tell the story well.

Let's clarify the term *presentation*. Although you may immediately think of a stage and PowerPoint, a presentation is any moment that you're delivering your product story. Your audience might be anywhere at any time.

You may encounter a customer serendipitously at a transit stop, have a conversation at a networking event, review your plans in an informal meeting, pitch an idea to a select few in a conference room, or deliver a formal presentation in an auditorium. Your message could be written, spoken, or visual. It could be delivered in a podcast, webcast, video, PowerPoint, tweet, post, or just about any channel you could imagine.

Although seemingly different situations, they all have similarities. The skills are the same and it's a matter of degree, intimacy, and whether you go big or small or somewhere in between. Whomever your audience, people want to hear your story as a one-to-one conversation.

Here's a secret: just by showing up, having a coherent presentation, and moving with confidence, people will put you into the category of expert. You are automatically *the Sage on the Stage* so use this opportunity to the best of your ability. Be bold!

In my workshop *Tell It Well!* I stress three fundamental perceptions about yourself to convey in every customer encounter: likeability, knowledge, and specific customized value.

Likeability is essential; first impressions count. Customers buy from people they like and likeability is often decided below the level of consciousness. You may have a superior product or message but remember that the customer is in control and won't be open to –and do business with – someone to whom they can't connect. Employ the soft skills of listening, empathy, and sensitivity.

If people like you they will overlook your shortcomings. If they don't, they will use them against you.

-Debra Fox

I buy my morning coffee from a local coffee shop. Here's a scene I witness nearly every day.

Everybody loves Hank. And Hank loves everybody back. He's an older fella who rings the register at a local coffee shop during the morning rush. It's a retirement job for him as a way to keep busy, stay connected, and earn some extra cash. With a friendly wave and good morning, Hank greets everyone by name and engages in friendly banter. It's easy to know when he's on duty because the line is long and moves excruciatingly slow. You see, Hank struggles with change and getting the orders right. Yet as he fumbles through coffee, croissants, and cash, his co-workers cover and the customers walk him through the tab. It's a community effort all accomplished with smiles, goodwill, and patience. If Hank misses a day, concerned customers ask. They'd rather wait a few extra minutes to be served a smile from Hank than get their coffee quickly without him.

Hank is the perfect example of likeability overcoming shortcomings. In the same way, if you're likeable, your customers will overlook the mistakes and gaps in your presentation.

Are you groomed, friendly, open, and in good humor? Listening skills are important because each conversation is an opportunity to learn; your best tool is to stop talking and pay attention. Remember, whoever listens most, wins.

Listen in an understanding and supportive way, pause before asking a question (to indicate that you're listening), and check for understanding. It's always a good idea to quickly summarize what you've heard, what you think you've heard, and ask, "Did I get that right?" It not only shows that you were listening but that you're paying respect as well as modeling a back and forth conversation.

Assume *positive intent*, that is, what you may perceive as hostility or disinterest may be anything but. On a personal note, my genetic heritage is Scandinavian and my light blue eyes are very sensitive to sunlight; I scrunch my face in bright light. On more than one occasion, I've been cautioned to stop glaring! A physical reaction to my environment is perceived as hostility. Cultural differences should also be taken into account. A *thumbs up* meaning good job in American culture is perceived as an insult in others.

Be aware of body language –others and your own. Facing someone with arms at your side and palms outward is a sign of openness. Crossed arms is a defensive posture indicating that you are closed off. At times you'll want to mirror your listener's posture to signal agreement and other times you'll want to lead with your own body language to encourage someone to your point of view. Control your rhythm and pacing, modulate your voice and intensity. As a general rule pay attention, be open, respond with warmth, and use common sense.

With a larger group, be sensitive to the energy of the audience –are they relaxed or wound up? Respond in-kind and double-check that you're holding their interest. Maybe it's time to drop the pre-packaged pitch and start a new topic. *Read the room* to gauge the level of interest.

I urge you to expand your *friendly* skills. Evaluate your wardrobe and hairstyle. Does your look convey the correct image whether authorative, casual, or somewhere in-between? Hiring an image consultant will help you develop your personal brand from the inside out (I recommend Kim Peterson). Department stores offer personal shoppers as a service to help create professional wardrobes that reflect your personality. Read a book on body language *(Persuasion Point* by Traci Brown is excellent). Learn listening skills. If you don't have natural empathy (and not everyone does), practice faking it until you make it. Mastering soft skills is well worth the effort. Above all, convey honesty, passion, and genuineness.

Knowledge is the second perception to convey. Demonstrate to others that you know what you're talking about. Are your facts credible? Learn what there is to know about your product from every source available. When giving summaries, you'll have the deep knowledge to back up everything you say.

Salespeople: demonstrate the product in action or describe how it works in detail. It's not about showing how smart you are –don't be a Dr. Know-it-all – but rather go into enough detail to demonstrate your level of knowledge and not the knowledge itself. Entrepreneurs: prove that you know your business as well as the investor's. Convey that you are up-to-date on financial, manufacturing, and marketing trends. Job seekers: don't just talk the talk but walk the walk. Validate past actions to prove that you have the experience and skills to be successful.

Value, specific and customized, is the third perception to establish. You need to offer a solution that solves your audience's specific problem. This is known as the *What's In It For Me* or WIIFM. Obviously, this desire is strong in people and at the core of most of their actions. Even when people are acting out selfless deeds publicly, they still want something out of it personally. That's why public broadcasting fundraising campaigns rewards donors with a Thank You gift. Even Superman, while battling mutant villains to save Earth from destruction, is looking ahead to a grateful kiss from Lois Lane. Find out what matters to your audience and discover that intersection between what you can honestly offer and what matters to them.

In today's marketing environment of multiple deliverables, channels, and audiences, it's a challenge to keep a campaign on track. Some organizations use a marketing framework to keep people, messages, and communications aligned. Some use the *Three Pillar* approach but I prefer the *Five Storylines* framework.

The Five Storylines Marketing Framework				
Core	Credibility	Experiential	Journey	Data
Maecenas porttitor congue massa.	*Lorem ipsum dolor sit amet, consectetuer adipiscing elit. Maecenas porttitor congue massa.*	*Maecenas porttitor congue massa.*	*Lorem ipsum dolor sit amet, consectetuer adipiscing elit.*	*Lorem ipsum dolor sit amet, consectetuer adipiscing elit. Maecenas porttitor congue massa.*
Product Summary				
Lorem ipsum dolor sit amet, consectetuer adipiscing elit. Maecenas porttitor congue massa. Fusce posuere, magna sed pulvinar ultricies, purus lectus malesuada libero, sit amet commodo magna eros quis urna.				

If NASA had used The Five Storylines Marketing Framework, it might look like this:

The Five Storylines of our Moon Shot

Core	Credibility	Experiential	Journey	Data
We're going to the moon and coming back	A relay series of rockets, space capsules, and lunar landers	Live television coverage means that everyone on Earth will be part of going to the moon	NASA is shaken to its core but bravely struggles on to ultimate success	363 foot rocket is taller than the Statue of Liberty and more powerful than 85 Hoover Dams

Product Summary

With our Moon Shot, mankind will finally go the the moon and come back alive. Using a relay series of rockets, space capsules, and lunar landers, two brave men will walk the surface. But they won't be alone as live television coverage lets everyone on the planet Earth watch every step and participate in the experience. We'll face setbacks along the way, men may even die, but we'll push on to success because the goal is bigger than one life. We'll have the hardware -our 363 foot rocket is taller than the Statue of Liberty and is more powerful than 85 Hoover Dams. We are going to the moon so come along.

Using the messaging framework as a guide, you can quickly create a messaging Bill of Materials (BOM) for the various channels and audiences.

For example, you might create a short, medium, or long print summary for use as a news release, web page, or white paper. Or you may be interviewed on television and need talking points. At a networking event you'll need an Elevator Pitch, for a speech at a technical conference you'll need graphs and charts. Remember that some people will need a top-level summary while others will need deep-level details. The possibilities are endless and the best way to put order to chaos is the marketing framework.

Too often, the messenger gets in the way of a message. Unfortunately, people will dismiss great ideas because of poor presenters. Good stories need great champions that are likeable, knowledgeable, and bring specific value to the audience.

Creating your Performance Persona

Every interaction is a performance in which to put your best foot forward. Your *Performance Persona* is a character that you create that tells your story well. The performance persona is the integration of your authentic inner-self with your outer personality. We often get mixed up when we think that our inner-self is on stage but in actuality it's our outer Performance Persona that we've developed. It's a matter of stressing certain attributes of your natural personality while suppressing others. There's no reason to be nervous on stage because you are just being you. Comedian Bobcat Goldthwait has an onstage persona that's loud and outrageous but offstage I've known him to be shy.

When I talk in front of a group, I find it helpful to think of myself in the third-person, as a character outside of myself who, coincidentally, I've named *Brad.* This gives me confidence because *Brad* isn't worried about my fragile ego and is more intent on the meaning behind the words. Try describing yourself in the third person and feel the power of that person.

Actors frequently create a *backstory* to their characters that detail previous experiences such as where the characters grew up, what clothes they wear, and why they like their eggs hard boiled but not scrambled. This exercise adds depth and robustness to their character.

In the same way, you'll create a backstory to your Performance Persona. Think carefully about your character's attributes. Confident, of course. What about aspirational, informative, entertaining, enthusiastic, or relaxed? Consider the physicality of the character. Is her movement slow or fast, stiff or fluid? Is his voice firm or flexible? Is their spine straight or relaxed?

The point is too create a vivid character that's outside of your protective ego and performs comfortably onstage whether at a social event, in a conference room, or giving a keynote address. If you falter, you can rely on your fully developed performance persona to get you through.

Sample Character Attributes

Character Name:	
Voice	Low, High, or...
Volume	Loud, Soft, or...
Movement	Large, Small, or...
Pace	Fast, Slow, or...
Physicality	Stiff, Relaxed, or...
Energy	Restrained, Demonstrative, or...
Gravitas	Authoritative, Peer-to-Peer, or...
Words	Complex, Simple, or...
Demeanor	Reserved, Open, or...
Other	

You shouldn't completely fictionalize the Performance Persona; you'll need the baseline of truth that comes from the real you inside. I once took a jazz singing class and learned that if my voice cracked or squeaked, it's because I wasn't singing from the heart in that moment. Jazz may seem easy but it's an early warning system for inauthenticity. In the same way, when you're delivering your story, if your voice cracks, it's because you're not being true to yourself.

Famous Hollywood actors always keep a real part of who they are in every role. Jennifer Lawrence will always be Jennifer Lawrence whether playing a revolutionary heroine or a ditzy girlfriend mixed up in a political scandal.

Vanna White is the letter turner on the American TV game show *Wheel of Fortune*. She is one of the most genuine personalities on television because who she is on the screen is who she is in real life. She's perky, friendly, humble, and real. I worked on *Wheel of Fortune* when the show came to San Francisco and had just entered the buffet line when I heard a commotion behind me. I turned to see Vanna standing behind me. I graciously offered to let her step ahead but she refused because that wouldn't be fair. As we moved towards the chicken and green

Public Domain Wiki Commons

beans, we had a very nice chat about nothing in particular. I was left with the conviction that Vanna White is the nicest person I've ever met –the same impression that she conveys on television. She keeps her essence while also playing a role. In the same way, always keep an element of who you are.

Knowing your personal communication style will help you communicate better with others. If you're naturally aspirational, work on bringing in more facts. If you're more logical, work on stories. I recommend taking a personality test to reveal hidden strengths with the aim of making your communication more effective through self-realization. A series of questions are asked and your answers expose personality and communication tendencies.

Most of the tests use a form of visual graph that assigns major personality tendencies to certain areas. Since we're all on a continuum, your position on the graph is unique. For instance, if you'd rather work on a project by yourself, you might be a task-oriented introvert (white star). If people naturally gather around you, you might be a relationship-oriented extrovert (black star).

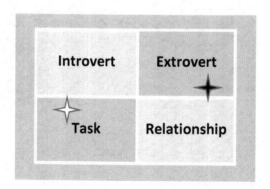

The predominant approach is the Myers-Briggs Test. In this system, I have attributes of an ENTJ, a less common type.

Myers-Briggs Personality Type	
E	Extraversion
N	Intuition
T	Thinking
J	Judging

Why is this important to know about myself? Self-reflection is valuable because knowing how I operate helps me know my limits as well as strengths which in turn helps me adjust my communication patterns to others to be more effective.

As an ENTJ, I naturally assume leadership positions, solutions come quickly so people look to me as an expert. The downside is that I move into the details before other people can catch up; I've learned to give others time to work through to the solution themselves.

We ENTJ's look at the world differently. If you ask other types to find a needle in a haystack, they'll detail approaches centered on pattern searches, sifting, or random luck. Me? I just use a big magnet.

Showtime!

All the world's a stage and all the men and women are merely players.

-William Shakespeare

Whether you're chatting over coffee, presenting to a small team, or speaking to an audience of hundreds, you're performing your "act." With the persona developed from the previous chapter, it's now time to hone your *routine*.

A tourist visiting New York City asked a native, "How do I get to Carnegie Hall?"

The New Yorker replied, "Practice! Practice! Practice!"

Pixabay.com

It's a really bad joke with an essential truth. The only way to get better at any skill is repetitive practice. A truism in stand-up comedy is to rehearse a joke until one is totally bored of it. Then and only then, is it funny.

However, you can perform old material while still staying fresh. I once videotaped a series of 15 TV commercials with country singer John Denver. Each one was essentially the same invitation to attend an upcoming show with the difference being the city, date, and venue. Mr. Denver approached each one as a new performance and, with a slight change of wording and genuine enthusiasm, kept his delivery fresh. To this day, I'm still not sure how it did it but I suspect that he had the trick of forgetting the previous performance and starting over each time. (Soap Opera actors do the same; if they have to go back and redo a scene, they'll need to re-rehearse the script).

Here's a few tips on becoming an expert performer:

- Create a blocking script with stage directions that plots where you'll move when, where you'll look, and your speaking pace.
- Set up chairs in an empty room and deliver your message to an imaginary audience.
- Gather a few friends and practice with them. Ask for honest feedback.
- Videotape and review every performance.
- Ask your audience to fill out survey cards.

We communicate in three ways: Words, Tone of Voice, and Body Language.

How we say what we say	
Body Language	55%
Tone of Voice	38%
Words	7%

Humans mimic behavior. By modeling actions and conduct, your audience will tend to imitate that conduct. If you want your audience to enthusiastically embrace your product, then be enthusiastic. If you want your audience to feel a heartfelt emotion (such as feeling empathy for a disabled dog), then you must be heartfelt in your presentation. Do you want them to think? Then be cerebral. And so forth.

Have you ever seen anyone smile while angry? It's difficult to hide emotions and the slightest mismatch will communicate that something's off; the body doesn't lie. Our body language and facial countenance are an expression of how we feel inside. A smile indicates happiness, a frown indicates the opposite. Don't pretend emotions but find a way to be real; the rest will follow.

Take Control. The audience will thank you. Audiences are annoyed by a speaker who mumbles, stumbles, and apologizes. You must *own* the room. If you don't take control, people get nervous because they aren't sure who's in charge. If you don't make yourself the boss, others will jump in to fill the void resulting in disastrous consequences for your message. Control the space by moving with purpose and guiding your listeners along. Confidently set the rhythm and pace. Speak from the heart. Be fresh.

Give Control. Have a conversation. Ask questions and pause for replies. Invite the audience into your story so that they become part of it.

No presentation is perfect; something will always go wrong. A slide freezes, a word is mispronounced, or a water pitcher is knocked-over. Don't ignore these catastrophes. If someone turns over a wastebasket, you can be guaranteed that everyone is paying attention to that and not you. Sometimes, it will be more subtle as someone entering the room late or a cellphone beeping. Keep track of where the energy and attention is in the room. When an interruption occurs…

1. **Acknowledge**
2. **Embrace**
3. **Take attention back**

A master at keeping control of his own presentation is Chef Jacque Pepin. I worked with Jacque on the PBS cooking show *Today's Gourmet*. The script for a cooking show is based on a recipe book that's been meticulously planned out, tested, and rehearsed for months before a single day of recording takes place. Every ingredient, portion, and technique is planned out to the last shake of salt. One morning, we were halfway through a segment and everything was falling into place like clockwork. Jacque chopped vegetables on the side counter while medallions of beef were slowly heating in a pan. Suddenly, the pan burst into flames and sent a fireball rising up towards the lighting grid.

Without missing a beat, Jacque changed the recipe and said in his wonderful French accent, "Now you must 'caramelize' the meat" which is chef code for burn it. Jacque acknowledged the moment, embraced the mistake, and took attention back. He turned a disaster into one of our best shows.

In the 2016 U.S. presidential race, Senator Bernie Sanders gave a speech in which he was interrupted by a small bird landing on his podium. The audience roared with laughter and, knowing he was upstaged, Bernie turned his attention to the friendly little house finch. The bird eventually flew off and Bernie turned the incident back to his story: "This little bird is a dove –asking for world peace and no more war!" The crowd went wild. *(https://www.youtube.com/watch?v=Jc2TVLoxsDA)*

Every presenter's worst nightmare is a heckler. They might be attention-hogs needing to be the center of attention, helpers with advice and contributions, jokesters showing off their cleverness, or anarchists disrupting for fun.

You must respond to every comment and interruption or you'll risk losing control of the presentation. Unless you're a well-seasoned stand-up comic, don't attempt the clever put-down because you'll escalate the situation or antagonize the audience. In any case, time and attention is being devoted to the heckler and not your presentation.

Yes, you want the audience to participate in a stimulating discussion. However, you need to make sure that one strong personality doesn't take over. Although every situation is different, the bottom line is to interrupt the heckler's pattern:

acknowledge, embrace the situation with an answer or a deflection, and take back you presentation. Sometimes, with a persistent interrupter, you can get other people involved in the discussion. Engage the audience to be your ally.

All presentations are delivered imperfectly but the good news is that small errors gives the speaker charm, genuineness, and credibility. Let your rough edges show; what you see is what you get. People don't trust a perfectly polished pitch.

The most boring rock show I ever attended was a Rolling Stones concert. Of course that doesn't make sense because it was a flawless performance by the greatest band in the world. But its perfection was precisely what made it dull; the concert lacked the spontaneous rough edges of a unique authentic experience.

Contrast that with a performance by guitar maestro Ry Cooder. To say it was a less than perfect show would be an understatement. Sitting on a rickety chair in an off-center spotlight, his guitar strings broke twice. Being a trooper, Ry chatted while repairing and tuning his strings. In the middle of his next song, the backstage phone began ringing and Ry worked "Somebody answer the phone, oh please won't you" into the lyrics. A wonderful evening because we, the audience, weren't separated from the experience by *perfect*.

Respect your audience. They've invested their time in your presentation so be grateful and pay them back with an entertaining, informative, and transformative experience that they'll remember for a long, long time.

The Seven Steps to Telling a Story

A good story is a journey through the brain. It's like a morning run that makes the listener break out in a healthful sweat as a result of satisfying exercise. Think of storytelling as *fictive motion*.

As a storyteller, you have a responsibility to guide your listener's experience so they become stimulated, engaged, and a different wiser person than before. For best results in any encounter whether it's a one-to-one, group, video, or stage, follow these Seven Steps to Telling a Story.

1. **Make a connection first**. Start with a familiar common context and let your listener know why you are there. Be clear up front about expectations. A comedian walks onstage and asks, "Where's everybody from?" The unvarnished truth is that he or she doesn't really care. They're establishing a connection through a shared moment and training everyone that it's now time to focus *your* attention on *my* act. If you take control of the stage, you'll have control of the conversation.

2. **Pay attention**. Don't assume that everyone has the same background and level of knowledge that you do; one size doesn't fit all. Through some subtle questioning, you'll discover if your audience is at beginner, intermediate, or expert level. Or a mix. In a presentation environment, the individual members of

the audience are there for different reasons; some are interested or curious about the subject, some are forced there by their employer, and some are killing time until the rain lets up. The level of interest varies: some pay close attention, some skim the material, and some are distracted by their own thoughts including tasks they could otherwise be doing.

People's energy rises and falls so be cognizant when the yawns start and eyes get shiny. People's expectations change throughout the day: morning is about familiarization, mid-day is productive action, afternoon is patient clock-watching, and the evening is devoted to relaxation and thoughtful review.

Ask yourself, are they motivated by logic or perhaps emotion? To whom do they answer?

With awareness, you can fine-tune your presentation to gain and keep attention.

3. **Stimulate aspirations**. People want a human connection. That's why they're listening to you rather than simply getting facts online. People want to imagine possibilities in a personal way.

I once attended a lecture by a scientist who droned on with facts and figures. At that moment, the only fact I was interested in was the number of minutes until I could get out of there. Then he related the story of how, as a young man, he hiked in a remote mountainous area and came across an ancient washout that revealed layers of volcanic ash. He wondered at the immensity of eruptions, the power of rainfall, and time. In that moment, he'd been hooked on geology and relating that story decades later, I was hooked too.

Your listener wants to go on a journey of the mind and it's your job to take them along.

4. **Calm with facts**. We live in an over-marketed world in which people have honed their skepticism to a fine art. People don't take things at face value, at least not for very long. That means that you have to offer *check-points* along the way with verifiable facts. Sometimes it's well-known trivia or other times a relevant but surprising data point. As the brain is immersed in a fascinating story, the logical brain is lurking behind the scenes to pop the bubble of fiction with the pin of reality. In the play *Peter Pan*, the audience suspends their disbelief and embraces the belief that the fairy Tinkerbell is real –if only we clap our hands loudly. But unquestioning belief only holds for a short time in a marketing conversation so our story must be supported by facts.

The belief in facts is powerful and pervasive. One day in my local coffee shop, I noticed a young family thoroughly enjoying their afternoon. The parents chatted amiably over coffee while the 5-year old played with a toy train set. As they gathered to leave, the mother said, "Oh that was very enjoyable. The banana bread was delicious and the coffee very good." In this instance, the aspirational emotional brain was enjoying the moment for itself, the delight of family time, while the rational brain needed to validate the experience with fact: delicious bread and coffee.

Be aware of the dynamic tension between emotion and logic. Above all, stimulate minds by triggering the aspirational brain with images and validating the logical brain with facts.

5. **Make them work**. Your audience isn't a passive vessel into which your message is poured. To truly engage people, there must be an exchange, a back and forth expenditure of human energy. Start by making the audience do something. As studies have shown, people retain more information from a presentation when they take physical action. People who take notes during a lecture retain more information because their hands are moving; they actually retain about the same as someone doodling cartoons.

   By having people do something physical, you're waking up their brains and giving them a reason to pay attention. If you're creating a one-way presentation such as a book, video, or speech, use words and images to make your audience work through a process; the brain will oft-times see a simulation as real. Show them how to behave in a situation. Or give them a task such as a puzzle that is solvable. Perhaps ask a question that leads them to an insight. Be their coach.

   Move your body, modulate your voice, and vary your tone so that you audience's brain will be activated, stimulated, and exercised. Inactivity leads to boredom and a non-receptive state of day-dreaming. The brain wants stimulation and if you don't present physical motion it'll create its own by drifting off into other thoughts. In any case, your listener isn't paying attention to you.

When on stage, give your audience's eyes something to follow by using physical mannerisms and movement –back and forth, up and down, and towards and away. Move into the audience to be intimate and back away to encompass the whole room. Establish areas on the stage and demonstrate clear changes by making a point on one side and a counter-point on the other to fully engage and exercise your audience's brains.

Some presenters deliver in a monotone voice and anchor themselves behind a podium which they use as if it's castle under siege. Do you remember any presentation like that? More importantly, do you remember what was said? Probably not because your brain went into a resting state in the same way mine does on a long highway drive through North Dakota. A straight road, flat wheat fields, and empty spaces doesn't offer much intellectual stimulation. When you're presenting, the last thing you want to mimic is Interstate 94.

Vary the intensity of your voice. No one can hear soft words so don't be afraid to use your lungs. On the other hand, don't shout the whole time as that makes your audience shrink back. The heavy metal band Queen never stays on full blast. In *Bohemian Rhapsody*, Freddie Mercury sings from soft to loud and back again.

Within your story, create a rhythm that has energy peaks and valleys. Demonstrate a playfulness between the left and right brain, between aspiration and facts. Keep the energy moving; build to a conclusion.

To plot out a presentation, I chart high and low energy points as well as movement from logic to aspiration. For example, in a PowerPoint presentation, I note where the energy is at any given moment and adjust appropriately. It's sheet music for my story.

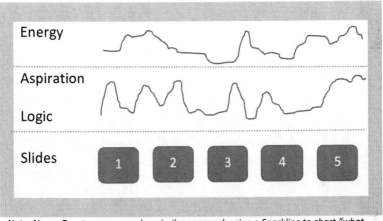

Note: Nancy Duarte recommends a similar approach using a Sparkline to chart "what is" and "what could be."

6. **Call-to-Action**. Too often, we create wonderful stories, engage effectively with people, change their point-of-view, create a desire for our product, and then forget to *ask for the sale*. Make a specific Call-to-Action and show your audience how to complete the process because, on some level, people want to be told what to do. They desire a call-to-action because they desire completeness. You aren't doing any favors by leaving loose ends; a feeling of uneasiness only damages your professional credibility.

   Let people know that you're nearly finished by reviewing and summarizing. Then, put an exclamation point on the end of your presentation and Finish Big! Make an impact on your audience by throwing out a challenge or asking a provocative question. Return to an earlier story and add a twist. Or tell a new story. Quote an apt phrase. Perhaps end with a video or strong visual. The choice is up to you and what makes sense in the context of your story. Give your audience something to think about and take along after the lights fade.

7. **Follow up**. The show doesn't end when the applause dies down, the conversation doesn't end with an exchange of business cards. Now comes the most important part of your story: following up. A great story will linger in the hearts and minds of your audience and your job now is transforming the glow of short-term memory into the crystallization of long-term memory and inevitable action.

Right after a presentation, visit with the audience. Be available and spend a few quality moments with each individual. Have cards handy and collect names with notes.

Then follow up. Within a day, make contact in a short email. A week later, send a survey asking if they recall certain aspects of your presentation; solicit testimonials. Keep in contact on a regular basis through emails, blogs, and newsletters. Follow up, follow up, and follow up. Don't let your story die from neglect.

Afterword

The Crystal Ball

The most basic of all human needs is the need to understand and be understood.

—Ralph G. Nichols

What is the future of storytelling? As digital technology disrupts traditional channels of distribution, it subtly changes the way that we organize our thoughts. Smart phones, texting, Twitter and Instagram have already changed the way we communicate and Virtual Reality opens up a whole new universe to explore. Interactive gaming challenges us to create story worlds in which characters act on their own. Audience expectations of information gathering is shifting from creating a personal library of knowledge to just-in-time delivery of specific relevant data.

Storytelling is evolving as new techniques emerge in response to innovative technological delivery channels. Yet at the core, stories remain the same because stories will always be how we make sense of the world and how we define ourselves.

Stories are forever.

A Final Word

It's every mother's nightmare. Your toddler, shaking and turning blue, is suffering a seizure and there's nothing you can do but hold him tight as you're rushed to the hospital. And like every mother, you ask yourself *why*? As more seizures followed that day, the next week, and the months after, it's a question that comes up over and over again.

One mother, searching for answers, discovered a study on the internet that linked vaccinations with Autism. A month before her son's first seizure, he'd been given the combined measles, mumps and rubella (MMR) vaccine. This had to be it. Relived but angry, this mom decided to take action. But this was no ordinary mom, this was actress and television personality Jenny McCarthy. She had a cause and she had access.

> *Without a doubt in my mind, I believe that vaccinations triggered Evan's autism.*
> -*Jenny McCarthy. CNN Interview, 2008*

Jenny McCarthy became the face of the anti-vaccination movement. Parents across the country listened to her and took action by refusing to get their children vaccinated.

In late 2014, a measles outbreak infected 51 visitors to Disneyland in California. News outlets quickly linked the epidemic to the anti-vaccination movement and a national debate was ignited. Emotions ran high as California instituted strict rules requiring all children attending public school to be vaccinated. Jenny McCarthy was alternately celebrated and reviled.

Then a new voice was added to the conversation. Philanthropist and mother Melinda Gates who, through the Bill & Melinda Gates Foundation, advocates health issues worldwide, spoke out about mothers in under-developed countries:

They will walk 10 kilometers in the heat with their child and line up to get a vaccine because they have seen death. We've forgotten what measles deaths look like. We've forgotten... the scourges they used to be. But in Africa, the women know death in their children and they want their children to survive.

-Melinda Gates, HuffPost Live Interview, 2015

Regardless of your position on vaccination, the point is that each mother used storytelling to make a compelling case. They've changed minds and so changed the world.

I challenge you to use Story First Marketing to make your mark. Use the tools you've learned to tell your story well. Remember, success only comes when intention and knowledge is turned into action. Continue your journey of learning by attending seminars, reading books, and researching online to become the best you can be. It's up to you.

What's your story?

Brad Cochrane

Appendix

Review Notes

- ❖ A story is a series of actions in which a sympathetic character confronts and solves a difficult problem while learning a greater lesson. The purpose of a story is to change the audience's internal state from non-interest to adoption of an idea; a story invites the audience to feel, be inspired, and act.
- ❖ Story First Marketing engages the audience through an emotion-based story in which a brand, product, or point-of-view is integral to the story and its completion.
- ❖ Stories are elemental to the human psyche. Stories are how we learn about the world and ourselves, how to cope, endure, and succeed.
- ❖ Narrative Non-Fiction are facts organized in story form.
- ❖ Stories convey the big ideas that travel well across all mediums, channels, and audiences as well as communicating to all decision-makers equally.
- ❖ The Logical Left Brain focuses on what *is* while the Aspirational Right Brain focuses on what could be.
- ❖ Data triggers two areas of the brain while stories trigger seven areas. Stories are better at engaging the human brain.
- ❖ Stories are
  1. Context
  2. Complication
  3. Result
  4. Lesson Learned
- ❖ Stories have action, emotion, character, rhythm, tone, and dynamic tension.

- ❖ A story has a structure that guides action, direction, and momentum to a desired conclusion.
- ❖ The Five Storylines
    1. Core Storyline
    2. Credibility Storyline
    3. Experiential Storyline
    4. Journey Storyline
    5. Data Storyline
- ❖ The Five Steps to Story
    1. Set a Goal
    2. Investigate
    3. Evaluate
    4. Create
    5. Release
- ❖ When presenting a story, convey three perceptions: likability, knowledge, and customized value.
- ❖ The Performance Persona is a character that you create that tells your story well. It's the integration of your authentic inner-self with your outer-personality.
- ❖ When an interruption occurs, acknowledge the interruption, embrace the situation, and take attention back to yourself.
- ❖ The Seven Steps to Telling a Story are;
    1. Make a connection
    2. Pay attention
    3. Stimulate aspirations
    4. Calm with facts
    5. Make them work
    6. Call-to-Action
    7. Follow up
- ❖ Success only comes when intention and knowledge are turned into action.

Acknowledgements

No one does anything on their own. My sincere thanks to all those who've supported and encouraged me along the way.

Tom Adair, Liana Antanovich, Wendy Baughman, Joni Barrott, Erica Beckstrom, Earl Bell, Julie Booze-Jervis, PMP, Lisa K. Bradley, Yvonne Brandon, Randall Broad, Traci Brown, Bridget Cameron, Frank Chemm, Sam Cochrane, Rick Dahms, Monte Enbysk, Charlene Fleming, Carolyn Fuson, Howard Hale,Devorah Harris, Jeffry Levy, Mary LaHammer, Tanya Houseman, Victoria and Cal Lewin, Neil Liebermann, Howard Liebgold, M.D, Steve McLendon, Media Jackals, Billy Mills, Caroline Peani, Sandra Piotrowski, Omar Rivas, Anna Roel, Janet Rosen, Bryan Rutberg, Nadeem Saeed, John Schoonover, Jen Semsak, Tord Skoog, Bill Stainton, Lisa and M3 Sweatt, Deborah Tahara, Sheryl Tullis, Karen Van Liew-Creek, and Brian Walters.

American Marketing Association –Puget Sound (PSAMA), IABC/Seattle, King County Libraries, LHH Executive Networking Group, Licensing Executive Society, Monroe Wednesday Writers, National Speakers Association –Northwest Chapter, Seattle Angel, Sno-Isle Libraries: Snohomish & Monroe Branches.

Special thanks to everyone who've attended my seminars.

Credits

Images are credited whenever possible.

Images from iStock and Shutterstock have been purchased.

Images sourced from Flickr and Wikipedia Commons fall under the Creative Commons License. https://creativecommons.org/licenses/by-nd/2.0/legalcode

Images sourced from Pixabay.com, the US Marine Corps, NASA and the Public Domain are rights free.

Derby the Dog and Madmen images sourced from publically available press kits.

Advertisements, trademarks, screenshots, and other works are excerpted for criticism and educational use under Fair Use provisions.

Permission for additional photographic images granted by Madeline Stuart, Rick Dahms, Mike Nakamura, and Brad Cochrane.

Graphic designs by Sam Cochrane and Brad Cochrane.

Egged On, Grok & Crick, Showdown on Flatfield, Cochrane's Story Table, The Five Storylines Marketing Framework, The Mystery Story Chart, The Five Storylines for Marketers, and The Conversation Map are original copyrighted creative works. Copyright Brad Cochrane 2016

Links

- ➤ **Derby the Dog**
    - https://www.youtube.com/watch?v=uRmoowIN8aY
- ➤ **Go Daddy – Cats with Hats**
    - https://www.youtube.com/watch?v=g5pnIH9ZB2k)
    - https://www.godaddy.com/promos/campaigns/cats-with-hats
- ➤ **Significant Objects: Kneeling Man Figurine**
    - http://significantobjects.com/2009/08/04/kneeling-man-figurine/
- ➤ **iPod Introduction**
    - https://www .youtube.com/watch?v=kN0SVBCJqLs
- ➤ **Chevy Silverado Hero Commercial**
    - https://www.youtube.com/watch?v=eZUNEhE-_Xw
- ➤ **Scope Hidden Camera Commercial**
    - https://www.youtube.com/watch?v=QVbWD0R1CPY
- ➤ **Ramune – How to Drink**
    - http://www.wikihow.com/Open-and-Drink-a-Bottle-of-Ramune-Pop
- ➤ **Subaru: They Lived**
    - https://www.youtube.com/watch?v=-oZcnH6uhLw
- ➤ **Bernie Sanders & the Bird**
    - https://www.youtube.com/watch?v=Jc2TVLoxsDA

Suggested Reading

- ➢ *20 Master Plots*. Ronald B. Tobias
- ➢ *The 100 Greatest Advertisements*. Julian Watkin
- ➢ *Aesop's Fables*. Aesop
- ➢ *The Artist's Way*. Julia Cameron
- ➢ *Beyond Words*.
- ➢ *Blink*. Malcolm Gladwell
- ➢ *Collected Stories*. Rudyard Kipling
- ➢ *Complete Short Stories: Mark Twain*. Mark Twain
- ➢ *Envisioning Information*. Edward Tufte
- ➢ *File… Don't Pile*. Pat Dorff
- ➢ *Louder than Words*. Benjamin k. Bergen
- ➢ *Made to Stick*. Chris Heath and Dan Heath
- ➢ *O. Henry: Collected Works*. O. Henry
- ➢ *Made to Stick*. Chip and Dan Heath
- ➢ *Persuasion Point*. Traci Brown
- ➢ *Pitch Anything*. Oren Klaff
- ➢ *Resonate*. Nancy Duarte
- ➢ *Use Both Sides of the Brain: MindMapping*. Tony Buzan
- ➢ *Winesburg, Ohio*. Sherwood Anderson
- ➢ *The Writer's Journey*. Christopher Vogler
- ➢ *Writing on Both Sides of the Brain*. H. A. Klauser

About Brad Cochrane

My personal mission is to champion storytelling and its power to change how people think, feel, and act.
                                    –Brad Cochrane

Brad's first career was in broadcast television working in every role from Executive Producer to Scriptwriter to Worm Wrangler on shows from Dateline to Roller Derby to The Young & the Restless. He's been a friend to rock stars, a warm up act for Governor Jesse Ventura, felt the wrath of OJ Simpson, and floated above San Francisco in the Goodyear Blimp. The one common element in all his adventures has been that television is telling stories.

Then Brad went into technology marketing in which he produced videos, wrote sales copy, and developed marketing strategies. The one common element in technology marketing is that facts and features are king.

Yet... the sales force wasn't connecting with customers through data. Decision-makers were no longer just the IT guys but now included CEOs. CFOs, and even HROs. Brad realized that something was missing.

Then one day, Brad realized this truth: *Stories are elemental to the human psyche.* To move customers to action, a new approach was needed that started with story.

From that day, Brad committed himself to storytelling by sharing his knowledge through writing, public speaking, and consulting. Help Brad spread the power of Story First Marketing.